"For those new to the Christian faith, Wesley Hill presents a moving biblical introduction to this climactic season in the Christian year. And for those whose sensibilities may be dulled by familiarity with the story, he offers an eye-opening, poetic account of the meaning of Easter, richly informed by close attention to the various biblical accounts of Jesus' resurrection and to the church's ancient liturgical traditions. An excellent resource for preachers, study groups, and anyone interested in pondering the mystery of the resurrection."

Richard B. Hays, George Washington Ivey Professor Emeritus of New Testament at Duke University and author of *Echoes of Scripture in the Gospels*

"Wesley Hill has presented us not with a single Easter lily but a lavish bouquet: scriptural narrative and liturgical drama, baptism and the church, Ascension and Pentecost, hope and healing, and a charge to bear the good news to the world. He wonderfully reminds us that Easter is neither an event trapped in the past nor a single holiday once a year, but fifty days of rejoicing the risen Lord in preparation for his final victory."

Sarah Hinlicky Wilson, author of *Seven Ways of Looking at the Transfiguration*

"'He is risen!' This is a joyful indicative than which none greater can be received, hence the Easter Alleluias. Words are not able to do full justice to what Easter commemorates, the climax of the centuries' long drama of redemption. Readers will nevertheless benefit from Wesley Hill's personal, poetic, and uplifting reflections on its Passover plot—the wondrous transformation of Jesus' death into new life—and on how baptism, liturgy, and the gift of the Holy Spirit enable the faithful even now to experience the first fruits of their new humanity in the risen and ascended Christ, everything they need for their everyday Christian mission of turning the world upside down. 'He is risen indeed!'"

Kevin J. Vanhoozer, research professor of systematic theology at Trinity Evangelical Divinity School

"Wesley Hill has greatly deepened my appreciation for Eastertide. He vividly illuminates the spiritual and symbolic elements of Easter, offering insights that will strengthen your spirit. I look forward to revisiting his work time and again in preparation for and celebration of this festive season."

Mark A. Yarhouse, Dr. Arthur P. Rech and Mrs. Jean May Rech Professor of Psychology at Wheaton College

"Christ is risen. In these pages, this first and fundamental announcement sounds afresh as good news. Readers are taken into the Scripture promises and accounts of resurrection, addressed with the gospel of the crucified and yet living one, and invited to participate in the church's festal celebration of Easter. This informed and honest study is finally a hopeful sermon and a joyous song: because Jesus lives with death behind him, sorrow and fear are not the final word, wrongs and losses will be redeemed, and the grave has lost its sting."

Jonathan A. Linebaugh, Anglican Chair of Divinity and professor of New Testament and Christian theology at Beeson Divinity School, Samford University

Wesley Hill

Esau McCaulley, SERIES EDITOR

Easter

The Season of the Resurrection of Jesus

Fullness of Time series

An imprint of InterVarsity Press
Downers Grove, Illinois

InterVarsity Press
P.O. Box 1400 | Downers Grove, IL 60515-1426
ivpress.com | email@ivpress.com

InterVarsity Press® is the publishing division of InterVarsity Christian Fellowship/USA®. For more information, visit intervarsity.org.

Scripture quotations, unless otherwise noted, are from the New Revised Standard Version Bible, copyright © 1989 National Council of the Churches of Christ in the United States of America. Used by permission. All rights reserved worldwide.

While any stories in this book are true, some names and identifying information may have been changed to protect the privacy of individuals.

The publisher cannot verify the accuracy or functionality of website URLs used in this book beyond the date of publication.

Cover design: David Fassett
Interior design: Daniel van Loon

ISBN 978-1-5140-0036-6 (print) | ISBN 978-1-5140-0037-3 (digital)

Printed in the United States of America ♾

Library of Congress Cataloging-in-Publication Data
A catalog record for this book is available from the Library of Congress.

30   29   28   27   26   25 | 13   12   11   10   9   8   7   6   5   4   3   2   1

For Solomon,

whose death and resurrection I witnessed at the font

Christ is risen! The Lord is risen indeed! So what am I supposed to say now? That cry is all there is to say—about everything! About our lives and sorrows and hopes, about the destiny of the universe, about ancient and current and future human history.

ROBERT JENSON

We are an Easter People and Alleluia is our song!

SAINT JOHN PAUL II

Contents

The Fullness of Time

SERIES PREFACE

ESAU McCAULLEY, SERIES EDITOR

C hristians of all traditions are finding a renewed appreciation for the church year. This is evident in the increased number of churches that mark the seasons in their preaching and teaching. It's evident in the families and small groups looking for ways to recover ancient practices of the Christian faith. This is all very good. To assist in this renewal, we thought Christians might find it beneficial to have an accessible guide to the church year, one that's more than a devotional but less than an academic tome.

The Fullness of Time project aims to do just that. We have put together a series of short books on the seasons and key events of the church year, including Advent,

Christmas, Epiphany, Lent, Easter, and Pentecost. These books are reflections on the moods, themes, rituals, prayers, and Scriptures that mark each season.

These are not, strictly speaking, devotionals. They are theological and spiritual reflections that seek to provide spiritual formation by helping the reader live fully into the practices of each season. We want readers to understand how the church is forming them in the likeness of Christ through the church calendar.

These books are written from the perspective of those who have lived through the seasons many times, and we'll use personal stories and experiences to explain different aspects of the season that are meaningful to us. In what follows, do not look for comments from historians pointing out minutiae. Instead, look for fellow believers and evangelists using the tool of the church year to preach the gospel and point Christians toward discipleship and spiritual formation. We pray that these books will be useful to individuals, families, and churches seeking a deeper walk with Jesus.

Introduction

THE PASSOVER OF THE LORD

Almost twenty years ago, when I was living in England, I got up one cold morning while it was still dark. I showered hastily, trying to scrub drowsiness away. I pulled on a heavy coat and walked down the steep hill from my flat, across the bridge that spanned the River Wear, and up another, steeper hill to reach the Cathedral Church in Durham. It was spring, but there was fresh snow on the ground.

As I moved closer to the cathedral, I joined a small but steady stream of other worshipers, bundled against the predawn frost, making their way into the nave. If anyone was speaking, it was in hushed tones. We were gathering for the service of the Great Vigil of Easter, the climax of the entire Christian calendar. I had been to many Easter services, but I was attending this one with a mix of intentionality and expectancy.

When we entered the vast, shadowed, silent space, ushers with small flashlights directed us out of the nave, the main sanctuary, to the chapter house (a windowless stone chamber where clerics meet), where we would sit in total darkness for a long series of Scripture readings that together recalled the high points of God's covenant history with his people. The service began with these words: "This is the night in which our Lord Jesus Christ passed over from death to life. The church invites her members, dispersed throughout the world, to gather in vigil and prayer. For this is the Passover of the Lord, in which through word and sacrament we share in his victory over death."

There was a reading from the book of Genesis about God's creation of the world. Another reading about the first human couple eating fruit that God had forbidden them and thereby plunging their descendants into woe and death. Another about Noah, the ark he built in a waterless plain, and the improbable flood that destroyed everyone alive except the small family huddled in the big boat.

I shivered in the dark.

On the litany went: Isaac awaiting but ultimately avoiding his father Abraham's knife, Moses throwing off his sandals as he knelt in front of the burning but unburnt bush. Reading after reading. Voices intoning ancient stories followed one after another, like ticks of a slow clock.

We arrived, finally, at the story of the Passover. God's people, the Israelites, had been slaves for hundreds of years, barely conscious of any honor they retained as Abraham's progeny. Maybe the fact that God had promised Abraham a land of their own sustained hope that they could still be released—but maybe it didn't, at least not for many. To this disillusioned people Moses appeared, announcing that the time for rescue was here. God had heard his people's lament and decided to act. God bombarded the recalcitrant Egyptian king with a torrent of plagues, the last one of which would, he promised, cause "a loud cry throughout the whole land of Egypt, such as has never been or will ever be again" (Exodus 11:6). The final judgment would be a visit from a dark, inscrutable divine messenger who would take the life of every firstborn in every home in Egypt.

There was a chance of escape, though. Moses relayed the plan God had made for the Israelites' protection: they were to kill a lamb, roast it, and eat it hastily (they'd soon be walking out of Egypt, so best not to sit down and kick off shoes), and smear its blood on their homes' vertical doorposts and the horizontal beam that connected them (which some of the church's most insightful teachers have interpreted as a cruciform pattern—the two doorposts featuring the blood from Jesus' pierced hands, the lintel collecting the flow from his thorn-torn scalp). When the angel of death saw the blood, he would know to pass by the house so marked and spare the children inside from the terrible decree. This experience of the Hebrew people—*pesakh* in their language or *pascha* in Aramaic and Greek—is the church's oldest name for its observance of what happened with Jesus on the third day after his crucifixion.[1]

After several more readings—the story of the rescued Israelites crossing the Red Sea, poetic prophecies from Isaiah and Jeremiah and Ezekiel, the last of which rushes hearers to a bleak valley of dry bones slowly being reanimated with sinews, muscles, and skin—we emerged blinking from the crypt and moved into an enclosed courtyard surrounded by four covered walkways. By the time I got there, the bishop was already standing in the middle next to a billowing fire from which an enormous candle was being lit and pierced with five grains of incense ensconced in wax nails, symbolizing Christ's wounds on the cross.

"The light of Christ!" a cantor intoned once the wick flamed.

"Thanks be to God!" we all responded.

Then the cantor chanted the ancient words of the Exultet:

> This is the night when you first saved our ancestors,
> freeing Israel from her slavery
> and leading her safely through the sea.

"Glory to you for ever," the congregation sang in response.

> This is the night when Jesus Christ vanquished hell,
> broke the chains of death
> and rose triumphant from the grave.
>
> *Glory to you for ever.*
>
> This is the night that gave us back what we
> had lost;

> beyond our deepest dreams
> you made even our sin a happy fault.
>
> *Glory to you for ever.*

Holding the enormous candle aloft, the cantor continued,

> As we gaze upon the splendour of this flame
> fed by melting wax conceived by mother bee,
> grant that this Easter Candle may make our
> darkness light.
>
> For Christ the morning star has risen in glory;
> Christ is risen from the dead and his flame of
> love still burns within us!
> Christ sheds his peaceful light on all the world!
> Christ lives and reigns for ever and ever!

We filed slowly into the nave and stopped at the rear of the cavernous space and encircled the baptismal font. It was large and slightly elevated. When the bishop stood near it, to baptize several infants that morning, he stood under a wooden structure that spiked upward like an ornate crown. Once the baptismal rite was finished, he took a palm frond, dipped it in the water, and swung it dramatically, showering us worshipers with cold droplets.

"Remember your baptism!" he thundered, wielding the frond like a whipped towel to quell flames.

Then we proceeded toward the front altar. Just as the circular rose window began to let in the first fingers of sunlight to touch our upturned faces, the bishop—finally—yelled out the Easter acclamation: "Alleluia! Christ is risen!"

"He is risen indeed!" we yelled back, sounding like an army celebrating a triumph. People around me took noisemakers—bells, kazoos, xylophones, maracas, and all manner of homemade instruments—out of their purses and backpacks. The nave suddenly resembled a football stadium, with whoops and hugs and smiles and cheers.

By this time, the rose window above the altar was ablaze with light. The bishop slowly mounted the steps to the pulpit. We all waited expectantly to hear what he would say. Only a few years earlier, he had written an eight-hundred–page book persuasively defending the claim that when the earliest Christians said Jesus had been raised to new life by God, they meant it concretely.

They really meant that the same person who had been killed and buried was now alive with a new, indestructible bodily life; the corpse that had lain in the tomb had been transformed and recreated by God.

"The resurrection of Jesus," the bishop proclaimed, "is the shocking new birth of a new form of life, a life that has gone through death and out the other side, a new sort of physicality that the world has never seen before."[2]

I recall sitting in the pew in that moment and thinking that, for all the bishop's eloquence, there was something inadequate in his words. How could human speech, even the most ardent and artful, ever do justice to the reality of that first Easter Sunday?

Preaching is good, but perhaps the singing that we had all heard a few minutes before was even better:

> It is right and good that with hearts and minds
> and voices
> we should praise you, Father almighty, the
> unseen God,
> through your only Son, Jesus Christ our Lord,
> who has saved us by his death,
> paid the price of Adam's sin,
> and reconciled us once again to you.

What I've just described is one of the most ancient ways the church has kept its greatest, most joyous feast day—the day of the resurrection of Jesus Christ from the dead, his passing over from death to life. "This magnificent ritual," one liturgical scholar has said, "packed with deep and ancient symbols, gathers into one celebration the essence of Christianity."[3] And in my experience, despite all the long centuries that have passed, it has lost none of its power to enchant.

One modern convert from an atheist background and now a priest in the Episcopal Church, Beth Maynard, has urged contemporary churches not to shortchange any of the drama and pageantry of the Easter Vigil. The first Easter service she attended as a Christian believer was the Vigil, and so, she says, she "long[s] to see more churches with the chutzpah to confront people with the sensory extremes this liturgy makes possible . . . night and light, silence and sound: honor these contrasts and they'll do their work on the soul with very little help from us."[4] It's inconvenient for officiants and attendees alike, but start the Vigil in the dark—either late at night on Holy

Saturday ("Sunset to sunrise changes now," said one of the earliest Christian priests[5]) or as early as possible, before the sun comes up, on Sunday morning. The deeper the contrast between darkness and light you can draw, the better. Maynard continues:

> A Christianity without adequate weight given to propositional realities would no longer be Christianity. The meaty themes at the heart of the faith—death, resurrection, healing, transformation, forgiveness, sacrifice—need to be studied and integrated intellectually through abstract and rational discussion. But they need every bit as much to be experienced with the body and the emotions, through nonliteral and aesthetic communication, in a context that marries them to the revelation God has given and invites our full-bodied assent through the power of the Holy Spirit. When we do encounter them in that way, they thicken gospel meaning, grounding it and enabling us to see how much more potent and elemental God's truth is than we might have suspected from our book-learning.[6]

Maynard's words not only capture my experience that cold morning in Durham, but they also suggest a more widespread principle: "The liturgy . . . exists not to educate but to seduce people into participating in common activity of the highest order, where one is freed to learn things which cannot be taught."[7]

There's an important sense in which a book like this is decidedly secondary. To put yourself in the place where you are likeliest to experience the terror, joy, and earth-shattering excitement of Easter, you need to go to church. But if you need some program notes, a sort of tourist's handbook that can help guide you through the church's worship, this book is here to help.

The first chapter will focus on the story of the first Easter as told by the four Gospels in the New Testament. This is the scriptural bedrock of the observance of the Easter feast. The next chapter will home in more specifically on baptism as the way we come to share in Jesus' death and new life—and what it means to return to our baptism on a daily basis as we learn to take in more and more of what Easter means for our present. Following that, we'll look at Easter as a season, not just a twenty-four-hour period. Many Christians have become habituated to the forty-day observance of Lent, but not as many are attuned to how the church calendar calls us to an even longer fifty-day period of joyous celebration and delighted feasting.

In chapter four, we'll look at how the lectionary for the Easter season features many selections from the Acts of the Apostles, underscoring the fact that Jesus' resurrection immediately propelled his followers into mission. It drove them out of fearful hiding and energized them to take the news of Jesus' triumph over death to the whole world through preaching and concrete actions of mercy and love, just as it does for us over two thousand years later. Chapter five will look at Jesus' departure from his followers—his "elevation" or "ascension" to a place and time beyond all places and times, from which he presently reigns as king at his Father's right hand—and how that departure is inseparably connected to his departure from the grave. Finally, in conclusion, we'll look at the final, fiftieth day of the Easter season, on which the church recalls the risen Jesus bestowing the Holy Spirit, "his own first gift for those who believe, to complete his work in the world."[8] Though we don't see the risen Jesus (yet), the last day of Easter, the Feast of Pentecost, assures us that he is still with us, to the very end.

The First Easter

Before anything else, Easter is a piece of news. It is an announcement about an occurrence, a short and shocking story. The earliest version of it we have, written fifteen to twenty or so years after the event it recounts, goes like this: "We believe that Jesus died and rose again" (1 Thessalonians 4:14).

The author of those words, a Jew named Paul, wrote a slightly longer version two or three years later, claiming that while it didn't originate with him, he could trace it back to eyewitnesses who would vouch for its veracity:

I handed on to you as of first importance what I in turn had received: that Christ died for our sins in accordance with the scriptures, and that he was buried, and that he was raised on the third day in accordance with the scriptures, and that he appeared to Cephas, then to the twelve. Then he appeared to more than five hundred brothers and sisters at one time, most of whom are still alive. (1 Corinthians 15:3-6)

A wandering Jewish prophet called Jesus—or "Yeshua," in his native language—had died and afterward showed himself newly alive to his friends and followers. That is the Easter story in its most original, most succinct form.

Several years after Paul wrote these versions of the story, a Christian preacher we know as Mark composed a slightly longer version at the end of a yet longer account of the life of Jesus. Starting with his baptism in a river, Mark told the story of Jesus' ministry and abrupt, clandestine arrest, his hasty, don't-look-too-closely-or-you'll-spot-the-gaps-in-the-evidence trial before the Roman authorities who ruled the territory of Israel with a firm but largely apathetic hand, and summary execution.

According to Mark, some women who had accompanied Jesus in his travels and seen him crucified went with some other friends to the place where he was buried. These women, Mary Magdalene and another Mary identified as the mother of James and Salome, "saw where the body was laid" (Mark 15:47). Within hours or perhaps minutes, the sun was setting and the Jewish Sabbath had begun, which meant the women were obligated to rest in their homes until the following nightfall.

Wasting little time once it was dark again, they took spices they hoped to use to mask the odor of Jesus' decaying corpse and arrived at his tomb as the sun was coming up on the first day of the new week. On their way, they had been troubleshooting an obstacle to their plan: How would they manage to roll the heavy stone away from the tomb's entrance so they could proceed with the spices? But when they looked up, "they saw that the stone, which was very large, had already been rolled back" (Mark 16:4). They went into the tomb. A young man dressed in white was sitting on the right side, and they became afraid. "Do not be alarmed," the young man said to the women. "You are looking for Jesus of Nazareth, who was crucified. He has been raised; he is not here. Look, there is the place they laid him" (Mark 16:6). The women could see that he was right. There was no body and no more need for the spices they'd brought.

The young man spoke again: "Go, tell his disciples and Peter that he is going ahead of you to Galilee; there you will see him, just as he told you" (Mark 16:7). The young man's words recalled Jesus' foretelling of this event earlier in Mark's narrative, but its meaning hadn't registered with the women or with any of Jesus' other followers, for that matter. No one had been prepared for this turn of events— if that's even what it should be called, there having been no earlier event remotely like the terrifying moment they found themselves enduring now.

It is interesting that the young man mentions Peter. Of all Jesus' disciples he could have singled out for special attention, Peter was the one who had, in the heat of interrogation at Jesus' trial, denied he had ever known him. At this point a question looms. Theologian Robert Jenson says an announcement like the young man's—a dead man is no longer in his tomb but has been raised and is now roaming his old haunts—is not obviously or necessarily good news. What if a stranger dressed in white announced, "Adam Lanza, the Sandy Hook killer, is risen"? That might be good news for a handful of violent would-be copycats, but it would not be good news to any parent concerned for the safety of their children. How could Peter—or the other disciples who had fled the scene at Jesus' arrest to save their own skins—be confident that Jesus hadn't returned to enact a bloody vengeance?[1]

Perhaps the women thought immediately of how Jesus was known, throughout the whole course of his ministry, for showing mercy to those most in need of it. Maybe that was all the assurance they needed that this was, in fact, a happy announcement the young man had given them. Perhaps they realized that the news—the unconditional friend of tax collectors and sinners is risen—was the most breathtakingly hopeful news that could be imagined.

If so, Mark doesn't tell us. His story concludes with a simple, awkward break: "[The women] went out and fled from the tomb, for terror and amazement had seized them; and they said nothing to anyone, for they were afraid" (Mark 16:8).[2]

The Gospel according to Matthew was probably written not too long after Mark's. For the most part, it sticks closely to Mark's version of the story, but it adds numerous details and makes a handful of significant alterations. In a scene that belongs in a horror movie, Matthew gives a sort of preview of Jesus' resurrection already on Good Friday, right after Jesus cries out with a loud voice and then dies. "At that moment," says Matthew, "the curtain of the temple was torn in two, from top to bottom. The earth shook, and the rocks were split. The tombs also were opened, and many bodies of the saints who had fallen asleep were raised" (Matthew 27:51-52). Jesus' resurrection isn't just an isolated experience, something we admire in his case but don't share in ourselves. Here is a hint that Jesus' resurrection is about others' too—a vital point we'll return to in the next chapter.

Matthew also notes that some of Jesus' friends—all women, as in Mark's account—were there at his crucifixion and again at his burial, looking on: "Among them were Mary Magdalene, and Mary the mother of James and Joseph" (Matthew 27:56); "Mary Magdalene and the other Mary were there" (Matthew 27:61). Along with Mark, Matthew names the member of the Jewish council who supplied an unused tomb—a small cave of sorts, it seems— for Jesus and made sure he was given a proper burial: Joseph of Arimathea (Mark 15:42-46; Matthew 27:57-60).

But Matthew adds a detail not found in Mark. Some of Jesus' opponents reason that his followers might come and steal his body from the grave and then falsely claim that he was alive again. "[This] deception would be worse than the first" (Matthew 27:64), they tell Pontius Pilate, the Roman official who had given the order for Jesus to be crucified. Fearing the spread of this pernicious rumor, they ask Pilate to allow them to dispatch some soldiers to keep watch at the tomb to prevent the possibility. Pilate concedes and then says to them, in what Christian leader and author Russell Moore has called the most hilarious line in the whole Bible, "Go, make [the tomb] as secure as you can" (Matthew 27:65).[3]

From there, Matthew dramatically diverges from Mark. He describes the women, Mary Magdalene and "the other [the same as Mark's?] Mary" coming early to the tomb on the morning after the Sabbath. But instead of seeing the dark, gaping mouth of an opened grave, they experience a sudden, "great earthquake; for an angel of the Lord, descending from heaven, came and rolled back the stone and sat on it. His appearance was like lightning, and his clothing white as snow. For fear of him the guards shook and became like dead men" (Matthew 28:2-4). Turning from the comatose soldiers, Matthew records the angel's words to the women: "Do not be afraid; I know that you are looking for Jesus who was crucified. He is not here; for he has been raised, as he said. Come, see the place where he lay. Then go quickly and tell his disciples, 'He has been raised from the dead, and indeed he is going ahead of you to Galilee; there you will see him.' This is my message for you" (Matthew 28:5-7). In response, the women leave the tomb in fear, as in Mark's account, but also now, according to Matthew, with a spark of joy, ready to tell Jesus' other disciples what they've just seen and heard.

And then they see Jesus himself. The encounter is sudden, unlooked-for. Matthew doesn't make the women the subjects of the action, as if by their diligence in searching they were able to force a meeting. Jesus is the one who steps into their path and says as they catch their breath, "Greetings!" (Matthew 28:9). One of the greatest contemporary scholars of the Gospel of Matthew has confessed his confidence in Matthew's report by saying, "I believe that the disciples saw Jesus *and that he saw them*."[4] That is the note Matthew strikes: Jesus, the one who is on the loose and goes ahead of his followers, makes himself visible to them.

Overcome with awe, Mary Magdalene and the other Mary "came to him, took hold of his feet, and worshiped him" (Matthew 28:9). Jesus says in response, "Do not be afraid; go and tell my brothers to go to Galilee; there they will see me" (Matthew 28:10). In the next turn of the story, the followers of Jesus have made it to Galilee. They go to a mountain Jesus had specified, and there they see him, just as the women had. He's not just a resuscitated corpse, he tells them. He has been brought to life to now be the master and judge of the whole world and the entirety of history. What that means, he says, is that they have a job to do: "Go therefore and make disciples of all nations, baptizing them in the name of the Father and of the Son and of the Holy Spirit, and teaching them to obey everything that I have commanded you. And remember, I am with you always, to the end of the age" (Matthew 28:19-20).

The Gospel according to Luke differs yet again. Almost certainly familiar with at least Mark's account and possibly also Matthew's, Luke tells the same story with a new and different twist. As in Mark's and Matthew's accounts, some women—which ones, exactly, Luke doesn't say—came to Jesus' tomb at the crack of dawn on the Sunday after his execution. They come bearing spices, as in Mark's Gospel. But they don't sense the tremors of an earthquake. They don't witness any dramatic, supernatural rolling away of the stone from the entrance of the tomb. They see that the stone has already been rolled away, and, going into the empty space, they also see that the corpse isn't there. But then they jump and scream (as I imagine) to find two shining beings at their elbows. They "were terrified and bowed their faces to the ground," says Luke. The dazzling messengers reassure them with a wry question: "Why do you look for the living among the dead?" (Luke 24:5).[5]

At this, the women go back—racing, we must imagine—to the city to tell the other disciples the news. For Luke, the entourage was large: not just Mary Magdalene and the other Mary but another woman named Joanna and "the other women with them" (Luke 24:10). But they are met with disbelief. Despite earlier indications in the Gospel that this eventuality was the divinely promised outcome of Jesus' life and death, faith in the resurrection isn't obviously the right response for the rest of Jesus' followers.

Except for one. After hearing the women's report, Peter leaps up and charges to the tomb. He stoops and looks in and sees "the linen cloths by themselves." Apparently this is enough to prompt at least some kind of incipient faith: he goes home "amazed at what had happened" (Luke 24:12).

Among faithful Christians of later generations up to our day, Luke's Easter account is especially beloved because it doesn't end there but goes on to describe an intimate encounter two disciples have with Jesus later that afternoon.[6] The two disciples are walking toward a village called Emmaus, about seven miles from Jerusalem, and Jesus falls in with them, although they don't recognize him. Their faces are downcast with sadness when Jesus asks them what they've been discussing with each other. Sadness becomes bewilderment when they realize this man doesn't know what's on everyone's mind. Incredulously, Cleopas asks him, "Are you the only stranger in Jerusalem who does not know the things that have taken place there in these days?" (Luke 24:18). He goes on to summarize: there was a prophet, Jesus, who aroused the ire of the Jewish authorities and was condemned to death by the Romans; then, a few hours ago, there was a report—confirmed as accurate by many of Jesus' company—that his tomb was empty.

Jesus, still unrecognized, chides Cleopas: "Oh, how foolish you are, and how slow of heart to believe all that the prophets have declared! Was it not necessary that the Messiah should suffer these things and then enter into his glory?" (Luke 24:25-26). Jesus proceeds to interpret the prophetic declarations—the Scriptures of Israel, from Moses onward—as foreshadowing what had happened to him.

At this point they are near their destination, and Cleopas and his companion urge Jesus to stay with them rather than continue the journey. "It is almost evening," they reason (Luke 24:29), and Jesus accedes. They sit down to eat, and Jesus—as he had done earlier in Luke's Gospel with loaves and fishes (9:10-17)— takes bread, gives thanks to God for it, breaks it into pieces, and gives it to them. In that instant, the light of recognition dawns—*we've seen this Stranger before!*— and Jesus vanishes.

With burning hearts, they return immediately to Jerusalem to add their story to the other testimonies. "The Lord is risen indeed!" (Luke 24:34). Right then and there, Jesus appears again. "Peace be with you," he says (Luke 24:36). Their earlier encounter apparently does nothing to diminish their confusion and fear, and they wonder if they are meeting Jesus' ghost. But he quickly dispels that notion by taking a piece of fish—and maybe also, as some early manuscripts of the Gospel say, some honeycomb—and eats it, demonstrating that his flesh is material and solid, not wispy and ethereal.

After delivering a commission to his followers similar to the one Matthew records, Luke—alone among the canonical evangelists—describes Jesus withdrawing and ascending into the sky where, as Luke's sequel describes, a cloud eventually hides him from the disciples' view (Acts 1:9).

The last of the canonical accounts, the one found in the Gospel of John, is in many ways the most intimate and beloved of all four. I say "one" because it is all contained in the Fourth Gospel. But it is not only one encounter—it consists of several accounts (like Luke, in this way) involving several of Jesus' followers.

John's story of Easter morning begins this way: "Early on the first day of the week, while it was still dark, Mary Magdalene came to the tomb and saw that the stone had been removed from the tomb" (John 20:1). John doesn't describe the mingled fear and bewilderment that no doubt flooded Mary's mind and body. He says simply that when she saw the opened tomb, she ran and told Simon Peter and the unnamed disciple "whom Jesus loved" (John 20:2)—almost certainly the eyewitness who ended up penning the Gospel—about what she had seen. Both men immediately ran to the tomb, but the beloved disciple outpaced Peter and reached the destination first.

Peering in, he sees the linen that had shrouded Jesus' corpse, but that's as far as he gets. He doesn't cross the threshold. That job is for Peter, who not only sees the same heap of linen but also a separate piece of cloth that had been on Jesus' head rolled up in a separate place by itself. (Unlike Lazarus, who upon being brought to life again by Jesus emerged from his grave still wrapped in his grave clothes, Jesus apparently left his tomb and his death shroud behind.) With some mysterious mingling of faith and lack of comprehension, Peter and the other disciple leave and return home.

But Mary does not. She stays at the tomb, in tears. Bending over, she looks in and sees two angels dressed in white flanking the place where Jesus' body had been.[7] "Woman, why are you weeping?" they ask her. She responds: "They have taken away my Lord, and I do not know where they have laid him" (John 20:13). (There is a special poignancy in that *my*.) Immediately thereafter, she turns around and sees Jesus standing near her, but she does not recognize him. At that point, he speaks: "Woman, why are you weeping? Whom are you looking for?" Imagining she is speaking to the gardener charged with the upkeep of the gravesite, she says through her tears: "Sir, if you have carried him away, tell me where you have laid him, and I will take him away" (John 20:15).

Then, in what may be the most affecting moment in the entire story, Jesus calls her by name: "Mary!" She turns again (does recognition require *metanoia*, a change of posture and perspective, not only for Mary but also for us?) and cries out, "'Rabbouni!' (which means Teacher)" (John 20:16). Perhaps at this point she lunges toward Jesus in relief and ecstasy, but Jesus rebuffs her: "Do not hold on to me, because I have not yet ascended to the Father" (John 20:17). The risen Jesus is on his way to the one he knows as "Father," and until he has been exalted and poured out his Spirit on his followers, it's impossible to hold or pin him down.

No matter. Mary's joy can't be hindered by Jesus' stricture. She runs and tells his disciples, "I have seen the Lord" (John 20:18). A few hours later, when the disciples are still huddled behind bolted doors for fear of what the authorities might do to them in light of Mary's news, Jesus miraculously appears. And what he says next is the key to understanding the meaning of Easter: "Peace be with you" (John 20:26). To the ones who abandoned him at his moment of direst need, to the ones who fled to save their own skin while his was being flayed, to his betrayers, he says, "Peace." Not "Now you've got it coming," not "Prepare to pay for what you've done," but "Peace."[8] Mercy for the undeserving is the overriding, hope-awakening theme of Easter.

As if to underscore the point, the Gospel of John records two further appearances of the risen Jesus not found in the other Gospels. A week after his encounter with his fearful followers, Jesus appears to another one of them who wasn't present for that initial meeting. Thomas is his name, and he has already told the other disciples, in response to their report of seeing the risen Jesus, "Unless I see the mark of the nails in his hands, and put my finger in the mark of the nails and my hand in his side, I will not believe" (John 20:25). Undeterred by this avowal, Jesus again announces, "Peace." And he says to Thomas directly, "Put your finger here and see my hands. Reach out your hand and put it in my side. Do not doubt but believe" (John 20:27). This scene has been unforgettably rendered by Caravaggio in his seventeenth-century painting in which Jesus has pulled aside his robe and Thomas is inserting his finger into the wound—healed but not closed—that was opened by a spear in Jesus' side while he was hanging on the cross. Rather than chiding, Jesus once again offers mercy, and Thomas responds by calling Jesus "my God!" (John 20:28)—the title the Gospel of John foregrounds in its very first verse.

Finally, the Fourth Gospel describes one final appearance of the risen Jesus to his disciples. One night, back in his native Galilee, Peter says to a small group of Jesus' friends, "I am going fishing" (John 21:3). They tell him they're going too, and together they steer a boat into the middle of the lake that had been their livelihood before they met Jesus. But all night long, they catch no fish. As the first pink hues of dawn begin to show on the horizon, Jesus yells to them from the shore, "Children, you have no fish, have you?" (John 21:5). Like Mary at the tomb, the disciples in the boat don't recognize the one calling them. They answer simply, "No." Jesus then issues a command (or is it a promise?): "Cast the net to the right side of the boat, and you will find some" (John 21:6). No sooner have they done so than the net is teeming with fish, and the beloved disciple—the one who had reached the tomb first—says to Peter, "It is the Lord!" (John 21:7). At this point Peter throws on his cloak and leaps into the water, desperate this time to be the first one to see and speak to the risen Jesus. Splashing his way onto the beach, with the other disciples right behind, Peter sees Jesus next to a charcoal fire, cooking fish and toasting bread. "Come and have breakfast," he says (John 21:12).

In the Greek of the Gospel of John, "charcoal fire" is one word, *anthrakia*. And this isn't the first time in the Gospel the word has appeared. In the early, cold morning after Jesus' arrest, just a few hours before Pontius Pilate will condemn him to be executed, Peter stands next to an *anthrakia*, a charcoal fire, to try to keep warm (John 18:18). Bystanders think they recognize him: "You are not also one of this man's disciples, are you?" One of them adds, menacingly, "Did I not see you in the garden with him?" (John 18:25-26). Peter feels his scalp warming, sweating. His neck prickles with fear. "I am not," he says—not once, not twice, but three times—saving himself at the expense of his Lord. Now, Jesus has come back to Peter at another charcoal fire, and—matching Peter's three disavowals— he asks him not once, not twice, but three times, "Simon son of John, do you love me?" (John 21:15-17).

Jesus rewrites Peter's story of cowardice and faithlessness in that moment on the shore of the lake. With a few gestures and a handful of words, he says, "Far more can be mended than you know."[9] That is the meaning and message of Easter.

2

"We Shall Also Live with Him"

In August 1977 at Holy Cross Abbey in Canon City, Colorado, one of the twentieth century's most renowned liturgical scholars, Aidan Kavanagh, delivered a lecture titled "A Rite of Passage."[1] It was a fictionalized recounting of a midnight Easter Vigil service in the early church, and owing to its vivid imagery, it has become a classic. I often read it aloud to my students, and I enjoy watching their faces light up at its drama.

Kavanagh tells the story of a boy named Euphemius who, after months of preparation and instruction, is about to be baptized. He has taken off all his clothes, symbolically abandoning his former identity, and is about to step into a pool that is something like a tomb. Here is what happens next:

The water is warm (it has been heated in a furnace), and the oil on his body spreads out on the surface in iridescent swirls. . . . The bishop leans over on his cane, and in a voice that sounds like something out of the Apocalypse, says: "Euphemius! Do you believe in God the Father, who created all of heaven and earth?" After a nudge from the deacon beside him, the boy murmurs that he does. And just in time, for the deacon, who has been doing this for fifty years and is the boy's grandfather, wraps him in his arms, lifts him backwards into the rushing water and forces him under the surface. The old deacon smiles through his beard at the wide brown eyes that look up at him in shock and fear from beneath the water (the boy has purposely not been told what to expect).

Then he raises him up coughing and sputtering. The bishop waits until he can speak again, and leaning over a second time, tapping the boy on the shoulder with his cane, says: "Euphemius! Do you believe in Jesus Christ, God's only Son, who was conceived of the Virgin Mary, suffered under Pontius Pilate, and was crucified, died, and was buried? Who rose on the third day and ascended into heaven, from whence he will come again to judge the living and the dead?" This time he replies like a shot, "I do," and then holds his nose. . . . "Euphemius! Do you believe in the Holy Spirit, the master and giver of life, who proceeds from the Father, who is to be honored and glorified equally with the Father and the Son, who spoke by the Prophets? And in one holy catholic and apostolic Church which is the communion of God's holy ones? And in the life that is coming?" "I do."

When he comes up the third time, his vast grandfather gathers him in his arms and carries him up the steps leading out of the pool. There another deacon roughly dries Euphemius with a warm towel, and a senior presbyter, who is almost ninety and is regarded by all as a "confessor" because he was imprisoned for the faith as a young man, tremulously pours perfumed oil from a glass pitcher over the boy's damp head until it soaks his hair and runs down over his upper body. The fragrance of this enormously expensive oil fills the room as the old man mutters: "God's servant, Euphemius, is anointed in the name of the Father, Son, and Holy Spirit." Euphemius is then wrapped in a new linen tunic; the fragrant chrism seeps into it, and he is given a burning terracotta oil lamp and told to go stand by the door and keep quiet.[2]

There is evidence that a liturgy of this kind dates as far back as the second century. It's no wonder, then, that another of the twentieth century's great liturgical scholars, Alexander Schmemann, has said bluntly that "the liturgy of Easter is primarily a baptismal liturgy."[3] The season of Lent, with its fasting and almsgiving, was a time for catechumens to prepare for their entry into the church as communicating members. Then, at the beginning of the great fifty-day celebration of the Lord's resurrection, in the darkness preceding the dawn of Easter, they would be inducted into Jesus' life—by sharing in his death. Baptism, you might say, is the way believers come to experience, not just assent to, the reality of Easter. And it is a vivid guarantee that Easter isn't just about a supernatural spectacle that happened to one person a long time ago in a faraway place. It is instead about a whole community of persons—Jesus first, but then also everyone who comes to trust him for their own experience of new life beyond the grave.

In order to understand that, though, we need to start farther back, with the Scriptures of Israel and the faith of the Jewish people. It's striking that the language of "resurrection" isn't prominent in the four Gospels' descriptions of Easter morning. The angels, of course, do say to the women, "He is risen," but there is nothing like what we find in Saint Paul's letters, for instance, when he makes the link between Jesus' resurrection and that of the entire people of God. In the Gospels, there is just the bewildering, disorienting story of discovering that one human being, not at the grand conclusion of history but in the ordinary course of an everyday morning, has come alive again after being buried. Why, then, do we use the word *resurrection* to describe it?

Throughout the Hebrew Bible (or Old Testament, as Christians call it), the God of Israel is depicted as the one who holds the power of life and death. There are stories of miraculous births in spite of infertility, such as Sarah's conceiving Isaac and Hannah's becoming pregnant with Samuel (Genesis 18, 21; 1 Samuel 1). There are also stories of individuals being restored to life, although there is no indication that they won't die again (1 Kings 17:17-24; 2 Kings 4:8-37; see also John 11:1-44).

Perhaps most memorably, the prophet Ezekiel has a vision of a valley filled with dried-out human bones. The Lord leads Ezekiel on a walking tour of this grim terrain, asking, "Mortal, can these bones live?" (Ezekiel 37:3). Counting on God for an impossibility, Ezekiel prophesies, and the bones begin to rattle and reassemble. Flesh appears on them, followed by skin, and then their lungs catch air, and the revivified army begins to breathe. From now on, says the Lord, Israel should never consider itself abandoned and hopeless: "I am going to open your graves, and bring you up from your graves" (Ezekiel 37:12).

But—crucially—by the time of the writing of the last Old Testament books, this metaphorical picture of Israel's restoration after being exiled in foreign lands has become concretely literal: God will not only give back to his people their ancestral homeland; he will even reverse death itself. The prophetic book of Daniel is the most explicit: "Many of those who sleep in the dust of the earth shall awake, some to everlasting life, and some to shame and everlasting contempt. Those who are wise shall shine like the brightness of the sky, and those who lead the many to righteousness, like the stars forever and ever" (Daniel 12:2-3).[4] The people as a whole, not just one widow's son or one desiccated army, will be given new life on the far side of death. Resurrection has become a corporate hope.

And this explains why Paul insists that Christian faith is ultimately the confidence that what happened with Jesus will also include us: "We know that the one who raised the Lord Jesus will also raise us with Jesus" (2 Corinthians 4:14). Although it took some time to work out, the original witnesses of the risen Jesus came to understand that Jesus' resurrection was the beginning, the preview and foretaste, of the long-awaited communal resurrection of the entire people of God. It was certainly a surprise that one individual Israelite would be the forerunner, but in the end, that only sealed Israel's confidence that all God's people too would come to experience what Jesus already had.

This includes not only us who are presently alive but also those who have "fallen asleep" in Christ: "Since we believe that Jesus died and rose again, even so, through Jesus, God will bring with him those who have died" (1 Thessalonians 4:14). Elsewhere Paul uses an agricultural metaphor to explain this connection between Jesus' resurrection and ours. Like the first ripened tomato in my garden that presages the delicious harvest to come, Christ's resurrection is the harbinger of ours: "Christ has been raised from the dead, the first fruits of those who have died" (1 Corinthians 15:20). Making the same point yet again, in what Robert Jenson has called the most remarkable trinitarian passage in the New Testament, Paul writes, "If the Spirit of him who raised Jesus from the dead dwells in you, he who raised Christ from the dead will give life to your mortal bodies also through his Spirit that dwells in you" (Romans 8:11).[5] Here is an assurance of our future resurrection grounded in God's action on our behalf: God the Father raised Jesus and bestowed the Spirit of Jesus on us, and that indwelling Spirit is the promise that what the Father did for the Son, he will also do for us.

Returning, then, to baptism, we can now better understand why the church has deemed it especially appropriate to include in Easter services. Baptism is a way of saying—through ritual and gestures—that our lives and hopes are bound up with what happened on Easter Sunday. Again, Paul is the first one who makes the connection explicit:

> Do you not know that all of us who have been baptized into Christ Jesus were baptized into his death? Therefore we have been buried with him by baptism into death, so that, just as Christ was raised from the dead by the glory of the Father, so we too might walk in newness of life.
>
> For if we have been united with him in a death like his, we will certainly be united with him in a resurrection like his. We know that our old self was crucified with him so that the body of sin might be destroyed, and we might no longer be enslaved to sin. For whoever has died is freed from sin. But if we have died with Christ, we believe that we will also live with him. We know that Christ, being raised from the dead, will never die again; death no longer has dominion over him. The death he died, he died to sin, once for all; but the life he lives, he lives to God. So you also must consider yourselves dead to sin and alive to God in Christ Jesus. (Romans 6:3-11)

Several points stand out in this extraordinary passage. In the first place, says Paul, baptism kills. Plunged under water, the old identity of the baptizand is drowned.[6] Martin Luther called this "the slaying of the old Adam."[7] Once, when I was attending an Easter Vigil service, as congregants were crowding around the font to witness the baptisms that would take place, I ended up standing next to a mother and her young child.

"What's happening?" the child asked, too short to see over the shoulders of the people in front of him.

What I heard the mother whisper in reply—what I'm sure she didn't actually say, but what I thought I heard her say—was this: "Someone's about to die."

It would have been a perfectly appropriate and accurate answer if she had said it. "We thank you, Father, for the water of Baptism," says the Prayer Book. "In it we are buried with Christ in his death."[8]

Second, Paul's language implies that Easter is replicated or extended, we might say, in our present. Coming up out of the water, the baptizand is a new person, raised from a watery grave and re-created in Christ. According to Paul, this means that even though we continue to move toward physical decline and death, in some mysterious sense we participate in Christ's risen life now. "Christians have already been resurrected," as one scholar of Paul's letters says boldly.[9] And this is why Paul says we "walk in newness of life," which he spells out even more definitively in his letter to the Colossians: "You have been"—even now!—"raised with Christ" (3:1). But there is also a future, bodily dimension to this risen existence: "If we have been united with him in a death like his, we will certainly be"—in the future—"united with him in a resurrection like his." The resurrection of Jesus is wholly definitive, whereas ours happens in two stages: first, paradoxically, we live out the Easter life in our present mortal bodies, and then, in God's final future, we will experience what Paul calls the "changing" or "transformation" of our mortal bodies: "The dead will be raised imperishable, and we will be changed" (1 Corinthians 15:52). "[The Lord Jesus Christ] will transform [our humble bodies] that [they] may be conformed to the body of his glory, by the power that also enables him to make all things subject to himself" (Philippians 3:21).

In the service of baptism, there is a "covenant" that those who are baptized make with God before others. "Will you proclaim by word and example the good news of God in Christ?" the celebrant asks.

"I will, with God's help," the congregation answers, joining their voices with the baptizands', remembering the moment when they stood at the font.

And the celebrant prays for the baptizands: "Grant, O Lord, that all who are baptized into the death of Jesus Christ your Son may live in the power of his resurrection and look for him to come again in glory; who lives and reigns now and forever. Amen."[10] This prayer serves as the starting point for life in Christ.

But as Martin Luther emphasized so powerfully, baptism is not something that gradually recedes from view the farther we advance on our Christian pilgrimage. "I am baptized!" Luther would famously say to the devil or to his own troubled conscience at any time when shame or fear bared its fangs, even many years after his baptism had taken place. John Calvin agreed: "All pious folk throughout life, whenever they are troubled by a consciousness of their faults, may venture to remind themselves of their baptism, that from it they may be confirmed in assurance of that sole and perpetual cleansing which we have in Christ's blood."[11] We return again and again— daily, Luther insisted—to our baptism, reminding ourselves that resurrection is our sure and certain hope, that

God will one day do for and in us what he accomplished on Easter morning.

In the Eastern Christian tradition, the most important icon of the resurrection—*Hē Anastasis*—does not depict Jesus stepping on his gravestone in triumph or blinding the guards at the tomb with his radiance. Instead, it features a scene that Western Christians tend to call Jesus' "descent into hell" or, more dramatically, "the harrowing of hell," and that we often associate more with Holy Saturday than with Easter.[12] Jesus is in the underworld, standing athwart a set of broken-down doors, their locks and chains lying at his feet like so much flotsam. He is surrounded by an almond-shaped aura of glory. With his right hand he grasps the hand of a bearded old man and with his left he seizes the hand of a woman wearing a veil. The icon shows Jesus, having thrown open the gates of Hades, snatching Adam and Eve—and, by implication, the entire human family—from death and judgment, pulling them up from their tombs as if to surge toward heaven with them. The point is vividly, powerfully clear: Easter is about Jesus, yes, but Jesus rises for all of us too. "For as in Adam all die, so also in Christ shall all be made alive" (1 Corinthians 15:22 RSV).

3

"Thou Wast Up
by Break of Day"

Already by the time when the four Gospels were being written, it was important to Christians to recall that Jesus rose from death on "the first day of the week" (Matthew 28:1; Mark 16:2; Luke 24:1; John 20:1, 19). Jesus had been killed on a Friday and had observed the Sabbath, in a sense, by resting in the tomb, while his followers kept the Sabbath by refraining from visiting the tomb until the following day. That day—Sunday, as we now call it in English—was the beginning of a new week, and for that reason the early Christians sometimes referred to it as the "eighth day," the next day after the seven-day week had been completed. According to the book of Genesis, God created the world in six days and then ceased from his work on the seventh day (1:1–2:3). If this was the week of creation, what could the "eighth day" mean but the time of *new* creation?[1]

Jewish Christians continued to gather in synagogues on the Sabbath, but there also emerged a pattern of meeting together on Sunday to commemorate Jesus' resurrection and to mark the day of the launch of God's project of remaking the world—"the Lord's Day," as they came to refer to it (Revelation 1:10; Didache 14.1). Each time they observed the Lord's Day, they would proclaim anew the mystery of faith: "Christ has died. Christ is risen. Christ will come again."[2]

It may be that the yearly observance of Christ's death and resurrection began in Ephesus with John the "beloved disciple." Orthodox priest and theologian John Behr has recently made a case for this, suggesting that the church John pastored kept the fourteenth of Nisan, the date of the Jewish Passover, as their time to commemorate the singular-yet-differentiated event of Jesus' death, burial, resurrection, and ascension, regardless of whether or not it fell on a Sunday.[3] Eastern and Western Christians eventually parted ways over when and how to continue this yearly celebration, with those favoring 14 Nisan— "fourteenthers," or *quartodecimans*, as they came to be known—losing out. Easter would always be celebrated on a Sunday and not on any other day of the week.

But which Sunday? Christians are used to celebrating major holidays on fixed dates. Christmas, for example, is always on December 25. But Easter isn't like that. It is, in the charming phrase of the Prayer Book, a "movable feast." It is sometimes celebrated as early as March 22 or as late as April 25. What explains and determines which day it will be observed in any given year? In order to answer this question, we have to go farther back and see how Jews determined when to celebrate Passover. Originally a festival coinciding with the first full moon of the spring season, its date was keyed to the vernal or spring equinox, the first time of the year (there is another time in the autumn) when the sun appears to rise due east and set due west. In many parts of the Northern Hemisphere, this spells the arrival of warmer weather and the growth of flowers and grass after the bleakness of winter.

New Testament scholar and Anglican bishop N. T. Wright recalls being at a party once when someone decided to read a portion of the seventeenth-century Prayer Book for laughs. The Prayer Book includes a table of numbers for locating the date of Easter with these instructions:

> To find Easter, look for the Golden Number of the year in the first Column of the table, against which stands the day of the Paschal Full Moon; then look in the third column for the Sunday Letter, next after the date of the Full Moon, and the day of the month standing against that Sunday Letter is Easter Day. . . . To find the Golden Number, or Prime, add one to the Year of our Lord, and then divide by 19; the remainder, if any, is the Golden Number; but if nothing remaineth, then 19 is the Golden Number. . . . To find the Sunday Letter, add to the Year of our Lord its fourth part, omitting fractions; and also the number 6; divide the sum by 7; and if there is no remainder, then A is the Sunday Letter.[4]

Wright comments dryly, "That speaks of an older age when clergy with a love for mathematics and railway timetables had more spare time than they do today."[5] But he also suggests that the movability of the Easter feast may gesture toward a profound theological insight: "It is gloriously right that Easter should keep us guessing, should jump out on us from behind the apparently locked door of ordinary time."[6] He has said that it baffles him why many of us should observe the forty days of Lent with strictness and rigidity but then skimp on Easter joy. We are invited to observe all fifty days of Easter—which Athanasius and other early Christians understood as a "week of weeks," seven full weeks of sevens, one great *magna dominica*, one long "Great Sunday"—by pulling out all the stops.

There should be no kneeling and fasting but rather one unbroken chain of celebrations of the triumph of the risen Christ. We are free, says Wright, to find a thousand ways to cultivate and prolong Easter mirth: with art, poetry, games, music, rich food, dance, and ringing bells. I'd add the traditional favorites to that list: dying eggs and playing hide-and-seek with them, roasting a lamb and serving it with mint jelly and plenty of delicious sides, drinking mimosas, wearing pastels, and displaying lilies on as many surfaces as you have in your church or home. "This is our greatest festival," Wright says, and we can enjoy letting loose.[7]

Many Christians have done just that, and some of these forms of celebration have solidified into established traditions. The first week after Easter Day, known as "Bright Week" in Orthodox churches, forms, with Easter Sunday itself, the "Octave" of Easter: the first eight days of the Easter season (echoing again the symbolic richness of the number eight). By the late fourth century, the emperor had closed the circus and theaters and declared an imperial holiday for the duration of this time, with citizens taking the week off work. They attended daily services, each one held in a different church, perhaps lending the entire experience a "progressive dinner" or "safari supper"–like feeling.[8] And they made enormous amounts of food, distributing it to the poor in lavish acts of generosity, sharing the excess of the occasion.

Sarah Puryear, a priest in the Episcopal Church, has tried to update some of these ancient customs for contemporary settings. She points to several enticing "theological cookbooks" with recipes that coincide with the church calendar.[9] The precursor to these books is Robert Farrar Capon's mouthwatering classic *The Supper of the Lamb*, which spotlights a recipe titled "Lamb for Eight Persons Four Times." Literally embodying and enacting Easter abundance, the recipe yields thirty-two servings of food from one leg of lamb.[10] Why not try it out at a dinner party, concluding the evening with a viewing of the joyous eucharistic film *Babette's Feast*? Or listening together to a joyous portion of J. S. Bach's *Easter* oratorio or George Handel's *Messiah*?

Many Christians are familiar with the so-called Stations of the Cross. If you walk into a Catholic, Lutheran, or Anglican parish church, you are likely to see a series of icons or small carvings set up along the north and south walls of the nave. Each one depicts a moment of Jesus' passion—Jesus' sentencing, his shouldering his cross, his meeting the women of Jerusalem, his stripping, his being nailed to the cross, and so on, continuing through his being laid to rest in the tomb. Originally pilgrims observed these "stations" in Jerusalem, on the Via Dolorosa, the "sorrowful way" from the fortress Antonia in Jerusalem to Golgotha outside the city gates, but they exported them around the world so that even those who could not make a pilgrimage to the Holy Land could still pray through them during Lent and Holy Week especially.

In 1990, during the papacy of Saint John Paul II, an accompanying set of "stations" was introduced in the Catholic Church: the Via Lucis, the "way of light," or the

Stations of the Resurrection. Although there is no official list, fourteen such stations have been observed, mirroring the traditional fourteen Stations of the Cross. Examples include the finding of the empty tomb, Jesus' appearance to Mary Magdalene, his breaking bread with two of his followers in Emmaus, his appearance to Thomas, and so on. Praying through these stations meditatively would be a wonderful devotional practice to take up during the Easter season; perhaps churches could host outdoor versions of them in church gardens or even public parks. Or as one devotional guide suggests:

> Stations might be prepared, either with images or perhaps with candles set in various locations around the nave, which could be lit from the Paschal Candle as the procession moves from station to station. [Or an] individual might plan a walk or hike, with various stopping points to read the meditations and with the time spent walking between stations for prayer and meditation.[11]

There is a meme that always makes its way around social media in my circles during Holy Week, when Episcopal (and many other) clergy are wearing themselves out planning and presiding at multiple services. It looks like a page of the Prayer Book, with a rubric (italicized instruction) that says, *"The Priest goes home."* Then there is a specified dialogue between the congregation and the celebrant:

> *People:* Do you have some time Monday
>   morning to get together?
> *Celebrant:* No.

But maybe this is where we clergy might welcome some of our limits and allow our parishioners to take the lead in continuing the party. We may not be up for coordinating any further gatherings, at least until the following Sunday, but the extroverted among us, at least, would happily join our family, friends, and neighbors in further conviviality and celebration.

The source of all these various forms of partying, we should remember, is the combination of our catastrophic need for grace and the sheer unlooked-for plenty of the grace that Easter embodies (literally) to meet that need.

"Jesus," says Paul in his letter to the Romans, was raised from the dead "for our justification," to establish a clean slate and honored status for us in the covenant family—us who were "the ungodly," the undeserving (4:5, 24-25). The resurrection is for all of us who couldn't foresee it and could never find a way to engineer it.

At the church where I worship, the custom at the Easter Vigil service is for the preacher, in lieu of writing his own sermon, to read instead the Easter homily attributed to Saint John Chrysostom, the "golden-mouthed" fourth-century preacher. The homily begins at the place many of us find ourselves at the end of the Lenten season: painfully aware of our failures, petty and otherwise; our betrayals and hurts; our jadedness and our persisting hope that it really all might be true:

> Are there any weary with fasting?
> Let them now receive their wages!
> If any have toiled from the first hour,
> let them receive their due reward;
> If any have come after the third hour,
> let him with gratitude join in the Feast!
> And he that arrived after the sixth hour,
> let him not doubt; for he too shall sustain no loss.

And if any delayed until the ninth hour,
let him not hesitate; but let him come too.
And he who arrived only at the eleventh hour,
let him not be afraid by reason of his delay.
For the Lord is gracious and receives the last
    even as the first.
He gives rest to him that comes at the eleventh
    hour,
as well as to him that toiled from the first.
To this one He gives, and upon another He
    bestows.
He accepts the works as He greets the endeavor.
The deed He honors and the intention He
    commends.
Let us all enter into the joy of the Lord!
First and last alike receive your reward;
rich and poor, rejoice together!
Sober and slothful, celebrate the day![12]

The imagery here alludes to Jesus' parable of the laborers in the vineyard. In that disconcerting or (depending on your location) hope-giving story, those workers who slide in at the last minute and work for barely an hour receive the same compensation as those who turned up at dawn (Matthew 20:1-16). For any hearers who despair of their track record, it's easy to see how this is cause for astonished, humbled—and very raucous—celebration.

My favorite tribute to this Easter richness is by George Herbert, a seventeenth-century poet who went from being a young man on the make to being the pastor of an obscure country parish. Originally a darling of the English court, Herbert knew well the genre of the *aubade*, the morning counterpart to the *serenade*, the lover's song at dawn for his beloved. But in his poem "Easter" he reverses the roles.[13] The speaker of the poem, instead of waking her lover with a song, discovers that he has already risen, dressed, and been out running errands while she slept:

> I got me flowers to strew Thy way,
> I got me boughs off many a tree;
> But Thou wast up by break of day,
> And brought'st Thy sweets along with Thee.

The meaning of Easter is what older theologians called "prevenient grace"—mercy and love that precede and out-shine any of our efforts to prove ourselves worthy. The poem goes on to picture our ambitions, moral and otherwise, as if they were the sun's daily efforts of coaxing scents from grounds and gardens:

> The sun arising in the East,
> Though he give light and th' East perfume,
> If they should offer to contest
> With Thy arising, they presume.

Creaturely attempts to rival the splendor of Easter, of whatever sort, always come up short. The sheer radiant extravagance of it all eclipses everything else:

> Can there be any day but this,
> Though many suns to shine endeavour?
> We count three hundred, but we miss:
> There is but one, and that one ever.

Here there is no "gather ye rosebuds while ye may." The buds are always bursting, and it is always Easter Day.

4

World Upside Down

On Holy Saturday in 2019, *The New York Times* published columnist Nicholas Kristof's interview with Serene Jones, the president of New York's famed Union Theological Seminary. In the interview Kristof, Nicodemus-like, tiptoes toward Christian faith with hesitation but sincere interest.

"For someone like myself," he says, "who is drawn to Jesus' teaching but doesn't believe in the virgin birth or the physical resurrection, what am I? Am I a Christian?"

"Well," Jones replies, "you sound an awful lot like me, and I'm a Christian minister." In another part of the interview, she elaborates:

> For me, the message of Easter is that love is stronger than life or death. That's a much more awesome claim than that they put Jesus in the tomb and three

days later he wasn't there. For Christians for whom the physical resurrection becomes a sort of obsession, that seems to me to be a pretty wobbly faith. What if tomorrow someone found the body of Jesus still in the tomb? Would that then mean that Christianity was a lie? No, faith is stronger than that.[1]

In the hours after these comments appeared online, I watched many Christians express their dismay about Jones's comments. It wasn't only conservative evangelicals who were upset. Believers of all stripes, including progressive Catholics and mainline Protestants, voiced their dissent. Here, for example, is how Andrew McGowan, dean of the Episcopal seminary at Yale, responded: "If Easter really meant just that love is more powerful than death but Jesus didn't rise, how's the love-death score today?" (The "today" in question was the day terrorist bombs killed hundreds of Christians in Sri Lanka.) "Is it coincidental," McGowan asked, "that liberal Protestantism grows in the soil of privilege?"[2] For those unshielded by safety and comfort, vague notions of love without concrete, bodily restoration aren't enough. What about the human corpses scattered on the ground like so many ragdolls?[3]

In Acts, after Paul and his companions proclaimed the resurrection in Thessalonica, some hostile hearers concluded, "These people who have been turning the world upside down . . . are all acting contrary to the decrees of the emperor, saying that there is another king named Jesus" (Acts 17:6-7). To many of those who heard it, the announcement that Jesus had been raised from the dead was an unwelcome declaration that their days of exploitation and domination were numbered. The Easter message was understood exactly for what it was: not a timeless proverb that spring always follows winter, but the heralding of a new king with an agenda to right the world's wrongs.

One of the noteworthy features of the Easter season in my church tradition is the replacement of the typical Old Testament reading in the Sunday service with a reading from the book of Acts. Normally (and appropriately!), we hear a reading from a portion of the Old Testament, followed by a psalm, followed by a reading from one of the New Testament Epistles, and then, climactically, a reading from one of the four Gospels. But during Eastertide, the Old Testament reading is suspended for a few weeks as we follow the narrative of the early church's mission beginning in Jerusalem after Jesus' resurrection and continuing, as Luke tells it, to the ends of the known world (Acts 1:8).

Why this highlighting of Acts in the season of Easter? An initial answer is found in the book's opening sentence. The author, Luke, frames Acts as a companion volume to his Gospel: "In the first book, Theophilus, I wrote about all that Jesus did and taught from the beginning until the day when he was taken up to heaven, after giving instructions through the Holy Spirit to the apostles whom he had chosen" (Acts 1:1-2). Theophilus is probably the patron who funded Luke's research and writing. Addressing him with an honorific dedication, Luke explains the connection between his two writings: The Gospel recounts all that Jesus did in his Galilean and Judean ministry of teaching, healing, and the rest, culminating with his saving work on the cross and in his resurrection. Now the sequel, it is implied, will narrate all that the risen Jesus *continues* to do through his Spirit. Though he has died, Jesus is now, in the words of one scholar and priest, "alive and at large"—on the loose, we might playfully say.[4] Though now exalted to the right hand of God, he is still active and dynamic on the earthly stage.

Acts is the story of the aftermath of Easter. It is one of the most striking pieces of evidence we have for the truth of the Easter proclamation: If Jesus had not appeared to his dispersed and demoralized disciples, imbuing them with new vigor and purpose, how could we ever explain their almost overnight transformation from a fearful huddle, hiding behind locked doors, to a barn-burning band of fearless preachers and ministers who were ready to defy the empire, if necessary, to take their message to the farthest reaches of human society?

The essence of the apostles' message and the meaning of their acts of witness (contrary to Serene Jones's and other modern liberals' outlook) is not that morning predictably follows night and that there is an inevitably hopeful arc to history. The apostles are too clear-eyed about the depth of the world's chaotic pain and pitiless injustice to attempt to trace an easy, sunny trajectory toward peace and healing. We should not forget that all the initial Easter heralds were Jews, and they were keenly aware of their fellow Jews' skepticism that a crucified victim of Rome's imperial power could ever be considered the long-awaited heir of the mighty King David. Though he lived nineteen centuries after Jesus' resurrection, the German philosopher Schalom Ben-Chorin could have been speaking even for many first-century Jews when he wrote:

> The Jew is profoundly aware of the unredeemed character of the world, and he perceives and recognizes no enclave of redemption in the midst of its unredeemedness. . . . This is the innermost reason for Israel's rejection of Jesus. . . . In Jewish eyes, redemption means redemption from all evil. Evil of body and soul, evil in creation and civilization. So when we say redemption, we mean the whole of redemption.[5]

Yet the earliest followers of Jesus sought to demonstrate, through their speech and their way of life, that "the whole of redemption" really had established a permanent beachhead in the storm of real life. The resurrection of Jesus, in their preaching, was not a pacifying metaphor or an eternal dream but an actual incursion of divine power into the middle of real space-time history.

The book of Acts explores two fundamental realities: first, the apostles' efforts, in the energy of the risen Jesus' Spirit, to carry on his mission in imitation of him; and second, the apostles' verbal testimony that what they did was in Jesus' name and for his sake.

Attentive readers over the centuries have noticed some striking similarities between what the apostles do in Acts and what Jesus does in the Gospel of Luke, as if the former are being deliberately portrayed in Jesus' likeness, with their lives taking on the pattern of his. For instance, just as Jesus raised the dead daughter of Jairus, a synagogue official (Luke 8:40-56), so Peter raises a beloved early Christian benefactress who had died (Acts 9:36-43). Like Jesus, Peter first sends the mourners out of the room where the deceased, named Tabitha, lies. Like Jesus, Peter uses a direct word of command. (According to Mark's Gospel, Jesus had said, in Aramaic, "Talitha koum," which means, "Little girl, get up!" In Acts, Peter turns to the corpse and says, "Tabitha, get up.") Just as Jesus had done, Peter takes Tabitha by the hand. Like Jesus, he calls together those she had loved before her death and presents her back to them, alive. Acts is about the life and ministry of Jesus continuing after his departure in his followers.

But it would be easy to make a mistake here. Trying to underscore this connection between Jesus and his disciples, occasionally Christians talk as if the only or primary thing about being a Christian were to imitate Jesus, to do the kinds of things he did. So-called red-letter Christians can pride themselves on ignoring dogmas about Jesus' deity or miracles, impatient to get on with putting his teachings—often printed in red letters in modern Bibles, to make them stand out—into practice. The only "creed" needed, it is sometimes suggested, is Jesus' double commandment to love God and love our neighbors as ourselves. But is this the meaning of the stories in Acts—that Christianity is all about our trying to spread peace and justice in the world like Jesus did?

The apostles of course did imitate Jesus, but they also insisted at every point in also *interpreting* Jesus. They didn't just act—they spoke. And in speaking, they turned the spotlight away from themselves and trained it on the one they wanted people to know and adore. They explained the source of their actions as Jesus' triumph over death as the long-awaited Messiah of Israel's God.

Early on in the book of Acts, Peter and John go to the temple in Jerusalem to pray. On their way in, they see a lame man begging for alms. Peter says to him, "I have no silver or gold, but what I have I give you; in the name of Jesus Christ of Nazareth, stand up and walk" (Acts 3:6). Immediately a crowd forms in the temple portico, astounded by the miracle. What Peter says next is worth quoting at length:

> You Israelites, why do you wonder at this, or why do you stare at us, as though by our own power or piety we had made him walk? The God of Abraham, the God of Isaac, and the God of Jacob, the God of our ancestors has glorified his servant Jesus. . . . To this we are witnesses. And by faith in his name, his name itself has made this man strong, whom you see and know; and the faith that is through Jesus has given him this perfect health in the presence of all of you. . . . Repent therefore, and turn to God so that your sins may be wiped out, so that times of refreshing may come from the presence of the Lord, and that he may send the Messiah appointed for you, that is, Jesus, who must remain in heaven until the

time of universal restoration that God announced
long ago through his holy prophets. (Acts 3:12-21)

Peter is not content to perform a good deed, even if
he knows it comes from God's power rather than his
merely human effort. He also wants observers to know
the *name*—the history and identity—of the one who
made the good deed possible: Jesus. And he's willing to
risk contorted syntax to say so. Woodenly translated,
his message goes like this: "And his name—by faith in
his name—has made this man strong" (Acts 3:16 ESV).
So in addition to focusing on how the apostles carried
on the work of Jesus, the story of Acts is also about recalling memories of Jesus and continuing to tell his
story, not just as the story of a concluded human life but
a human life that is ongoing and capable of changing
current events.

In his classic introduction to the Christian faith, *Basic
Christianity*, written in 1958, the Anglican preacher John
Stott wrote:

The most striking feature of the teaching of Jesus is
that he was constantly talking about himself. It is
true that he spoke much about the fatherhood of

God and the kingdom of God. But then he added
that he was the Father's "Son," and that he had come
to inaugurate the kingdom. Entry into the kingdom
depended on [people]'s response to him. He even
did not hesitate to call the kingdom of God "my
kingdom." This self-centeredness of the teaching of
Jesus immediately sets him apart from the other
great religious teachers of the world. They were self-
effacing. He was self-advancing. They pointed men
away from themselves, saying, "This is the truth, so
far as I perceive it; follow that." Jesus said, "I am the
truth; follow me." The founder of none of the ethnic
religions ever dared to say such a thing. . . . The
great question to which . . . [Jesus'] teaching led
was, "Who do you say that I am?"[6]

The post-Easter mission of the apostles, as Acts describes
it, was the effort to keep that question alive and urgent
wherever they went.

The organization that John Stott helped steer, the Lausanne Committee for World Evangelization, issued a

groundbreaking statement in 1974 that "affirm[ed] that evangelism and socio-political involvement are both part of our Christian duty."[7] As Stott would later put it, commenting on the statement:

> It is our duty to be involved in socio-political action; that is, both in social action (caring for society's casualties) and in political action (concerned for the structures of society itself). For both active evangelistic and social involvement are necessary expressions of . . . our obedience to Jesus Christ.[8]

The same Jesus who called his followers to reject the love of money, cast out demonic oppressors, and proclaim freedom to the captives is now alive again on the other side of death. He has commanded that forgiveness of sins be preached in his name, and at the same time he has called us to participate in the spread of his liberating kingdom.

Several decades before the meeting of the Lausanne Committee, in a different corner of the Anglican Church that she shared with Stott, a writer and activist named Vida Dutton Scudder also underscored these twin themes of the book of Acts. Scudder grew up as a "missionary kid" (her parents served the church in India before her father's tragic death) and later went on to study in Oxford, where she encountered the progressive ideals of the social critic John Ruskin and worked briefly for the Salvation Army. Eventually she moved back to the States and encouraged middle-class Christians to move into poor neighborhoods, in a sort of precursor to the Christian Community Development Association pioneered by the civil rights activist John Perkins.[9] She ended up founding the Church of the Carpenter in Boston, a congregation aiming to unite the working class with more upwardly mobile Christians in worship and witness.

In 1918, Scudder delivered some lectures on the social implications of the church calendar, later published as *Social Teachings of the Christian Year*.[10] She recommended reading these reflections with an open Bible and a copy of the Book of Common Prayer within easy reach. In the lecture on the season of Easter, she squarely faced what she took to be one of the strongest objections to Easter faith: that by telling the story of a divine Savior who escapes the clutches of death and is whisked away to an eternal home, Easter encourages indifference to the concrete injustices and responsibilities of the here and now. Isn't Easter just a pie-in-the-sky fantasy that steals our precious attention away from areas where we could make a real difference in alleviating human suffering in the present?

In response, Scudder notes that the Gospel accounts of Jesus' post-resurrection appearances record nothing of any visionary reports from beyond the grave. Easter isn't about fleeing the real world. On the contrary, it is as if, now having death behind him, Jesus is all the more bent on reclaiming what he had cared about in his earthly life. His instructions to his followers in the forty days between his resurrection and ascension, says Scudder, were about "training his followers to create the Beloved Community":

> We associate the teaching of the Kingdom with the bright times of the earthly ministry, and easily forget that it belongs just as much to these last mystical phases of Christ's intercourse with his disciples. Yet it does. This is the purpose He entrusts to them, this the Gospel which they are to carry to the uttermost ends of the earth. . . . What He gave them to

transmit was the old Gospel, the Good News, the glad tidings, preached first of all to the poor.[11]

Far from endorsing an escapist etherealism, Easter faith fuels social activism. According to Scudder, the immortality brought to life and light on Easter morning "is the creed of social hope."[12]

5

The Right Hand of God

In the Acts of the Apostles, Luke tells us that Jesus, after his suffering and death, "presented himself alive to [his followers] by many convincing proofs, appearing to them during forty days and speaking about the kingdom of God" (1:3). At the conclusion of that forty-day period, Luke says, the earthly appearances of Jesus came to an end, when "as they were watching, he was lifted up, and a cloud took him out of their sight" (1:9). Jesus' disciples continued to gaze up into the sky,[1] and "suddenly two men in white robes stood by them. They said, 'Men of Galilee, why do you stand looking up toward heaven? This Jesus, who has been taken up from you into heaven, will come in the same way as you saw him go into heaven'" (1:10-11). And so, as we now recite in the creed, Jesus "ascended into heaven."

One of the high points of Eastertide is the church's remembrance of this event. For Orthodox Christians, the Feast of the Ascension marks the conclusion of the Easter season. Western Christians, Catholic and Protestant, extend the season for ten more days, until the day of Pentecost (which we'll discuss in the conclusion), though they also attach special significance to the ascension. In my tradition, we observe the day with a Thursday service, often held in the evening, in which we pray:

> Almighty God, whose blessed Son our Savior Jesus Christ ascended far above all heavens that he might fill all things: Mercifully give us faith to perceive that, according to his promise, he abides with his Church on earth, even to the end of the ages; through Jesus Christ our Lord, who lives and reigns with you and the Holy Spirit, one God, in glory everlasting. Amen.[2]

Ascension Day, however, is often downplayed or even overlooked in otherwise calendar-conscious churches. "Of all the articles in the creed," said one Anglican priest, "there is none that has been so neglected . . . as that which affirms our Lord's Ascension into heaven."[3] In an essay titled "The Call to Be Formed and Transformed by the Spirit of the Ascended Christ," the late theologian Marva Dawn encouraged churches, especially those not inclined to emphasize less-talked-about feasts, "to restore Ascension Day as a major church holy day": "Ascension is a deep symbol that people don't understand anymore because we so rarely discuss it."[4]

Then there are those who do understand the symbol but remain bewildered or embarrassed by it, given the awkwardness and difficulty of attempts to reconcile the story Luke tells with what we moderns know about the makeup of the universe. I was once teaching a Sunday school class on the meaning of the ascension, and one of my parishioners said, with full seriousness, "There must have been a divine spaceship or something that Jesus flew into, because it's impossible for humans to breathe in outer space!"

Another acquaintance of mine, after visiting the Mount of Olives in Jerusalem and seeing the "Ascension Rock," which features a fossilized footprint ("as if [Jesus] sprang into the heavens with such vigour that the very rock underneath his feet was compressed in the act!"[5]), joked with me about his reaction: "Jesus actually *ascended?* Right here from this rocky outcrop? Next thing I know, I'm supposed to believe he was wearing a cape and a superhero mask!" How then should modern Western Christians think about this event? What does it mean to keep this feast not only with reverence but faithful understanding?

We should first say what observance of the ascension should not involve. It shouldn't be understood as a simple continuation of Jesus' earthly life—as if it were now time for a sequel to the Gospels, "The further adventures of Jesus Christ," so to speak, or "Travels in Galilee, part two: from there to outer space." The Catholic priest James Alison has suggested a thought experiment: suppose Jesus' birthday had been on Holy Saturday, the day on which he lay dead in the tomb. Would it be the case that if he were thirty-three on Good Friday, he would be thirty-four when he rose on Easter Sunday? No, says Alison: "For Jesus, the resurrection was the giving back of the whole of his human life, leading up to, and including his death. It was not simply the next stage in his human life."[6] Or as the New Testament scholar Luke Timothy Johnson has put it,

The Christian claim concerning the resurrection of Jesus is not that he picked up his old manner of life, but rather that after his death he entered into an entirely new form of existence, one in which he shared the power of God and in which he could share that power with others.[7]

We have to try to free ourselves from any crudely realistic picture. Jesus was not merely resuscitated so he could carry on living in the same way he had before. We shouldn't imagine that if we had a rocket sufficiently powerful, for example, we might be able to reach Jesus somewhere in a remote galaxy and find out what he's been up to in the meantime. "When Christ sat on the right hand of the Father," quipped the church father Athanasius, "he did not put the Father on his left."[8]

This is perhaps a good place to underscore the important distinction between *resuscitation* and *resurrection*. There are several joyous and intriguing "resurrection-like" events in the New Testament, several of which we have already mentioned: Jesus' raising of Lazarus from the dead in John chapter 11, for example, or Peter's raising Tabitha in the power of Jesus' name in the book of Acts. These stories are powerful indicators of God's power over death, and in that way, they point to the reality of the resurrection. Yet they also need to be distinguished from what happened with Jesus on Easter morning. These stories of resuscitation are about people being snatched from the clutches of death so they could enter afresh into the lives they enjoyed on earth. Presumably—and painfully—they would have had to undergo death a second time at some point in the following years. This is why as a child I concluded that I would not have wanted to be Lazarus! Dying once is enough. Crucially, this is not the meaning of Easter. Jesus was raised in such a way that he can say, in his ascended glory, "I was dead, and see, I am alive forever and ever" (Revelation 1:18). He now lives with death definitively behind him.

A related misunderstanding we should guard against is that Jesus somehow underwent a character transformation when he rose and ascended, as if he exchanged the mercy and tenderness that marked his earthly ministry for a sterner, more impatient demeanor now that he is no longer bound by time and space. No, says Peter in his sermon on the day of Pentecost, "This Jesus"—the same one you heard and saw, the one who was killed in Jerusalem—"God raised up" (Acts 2:32). The ascension doesn't mean we're now left to puzzle out a wholly new personality and discern whether we can trust his intentions. It means instead that the Jesus we see in the Gospels, the friend of prostitutes and lepers, is now the ruler and judge of all things.

So much for what the ascension doesn't mean. But how should we interpret it positively? What is its significance for our faith and its import for a better understanding of the season of Easter? Perhaps paradoxically, one of the best places to look for an answer to these questions is the Gospel according to John. Even though John, unlike Luke, does not narrate the event, he imbues the ascension with more meaning and drama than any of the other Gospels. Right after John describes Jesus' miraculous feeding of the five thousand and his declaration that he himself is the bread that has come down, manna-like, from heaven, Jesus' followers are bewildered. "Does this [teaching] offend you?" he asks. "Then what if you were to see the Son of Man ascending to where he was before?" (John 6:61-62).

Jesus is talking about himself here in the third person, using an idiom from Israel's Scripture that means "a human being" or "a mortal": he is the human one who will return to the source of his life, the one he called Father. But if we hear the resonances of the Old Testament echo, we can also detect a deeper meaning. In the book of Daniel, which Jesus was apparently drawing on, the prophet has a vision of God's heavenly court, in which God himself appears as an Ancient One sitting on a throne made of fire. Throngs of messengers attend him, and the final judgment of history commences. "As I watched in the night visions," Daniel reports,

> I saw one like a son of man coming with the clouds of heaven. And he came to the Ancient One and was presented before him. To him was given dominion and glory and kingship, that all peoples, nations, and languages should serve him. His dominion is an everlasting dominion that shall not pass away, and his kingship is one that shall never be destroyed. (Daniel 7:13-14)

Into the divine courtroom comes a human figure, riding on clouds. He stands in front of the throne and receives his right to rule. For the prophet and his original hearers, this "son of man" symbolized the people of Israel. They were meant to carry on Adam's task of stewarding and ruling over God's good creation. As one psalmist put it, "You have given them dominion over the works of your hands; you have put all things under their feet" (Psalm 8:6). But Jesus seems to concentrate the imagery and focus it singularly on himself. He is, we might say, the representative Israelite. His ascension to his Father's right hand is what the prophet had seen dimly in his vision.[9] He has summed up Israel's vocation in his life, death, and resurrection, and now the ascension means he reigns over all things with the authority of God himself.

Furthermore, John's Gospel hints that the ascension has meaning for human existence as such, not only for Israel's specific role. After Easter, Jesus invites Thomas to see that he really is still recognizable as a human being; he has the scars to prove it. Later, it is implied that he shares bread and fish with his disciples on the lakeshore. Whatever else his risen life involves, he is still apprehensible in bodily form. He has vocal cords with which he speaks the names of his followers. He has wounds that can be touched and a belly that can digest breakfast. At the same time, when Mary Magdalene encounters Jesus near his tomb on Easter morning, he tells her not to try to relate to him in the same way she always had: "Do not hold on to me, because I have not yet ascended to the Father" (John 20:17). Here we have a clear pointer to what N. T. Wright has called Jesus' "transphysicality"— the way his risen existence is still physical, still very much human, but in a wholly new form.[10]

"Jesus's resurrected flesh," Paul Griffiths speculates, "is dazzlingly dangerous; and attempts to hold on to it, to keep it where it is by placing it in tabernacle tents, or by grasping it, offend against its nature. It is on its way somewhere."[11] Jesus is bearing his risen flesh to the Father. As he is exalted and glorified, so, he says, will we be in his wake: "If I go and prepare a place for you, I will come again and will take you to myself, so that where I am, there you may be also" (John 14:3). As we sing in the hymn, "Made like him, like him we rise, / ours the cross, the grave, the skies."[12]

Or to put it the other way around, the ascension validates our human existence by honoring Jesus'. Since our human nature matters to God, he exalts Jesus as our forerunner, our champion and pioneer. Our humanity is the humanity that he now presents to the Father. Might that sandal-sized depression in the Olivet rock still be, then, "even for the new millennium, a symbol of that steadfast devotion to particularity—the particularity of the God of Israel and of Jesus the Christ"—a particularity that includes all of us whom he represents?[13]

Many Christians, perhaps without thinking too much about it, assume that when Jesus ascended into heaven, he entered into a kind of spiritual existence with no more need for his physical body. Even those of us, like me, who were raised in orthodox Christian churches probably harbor some notion of eternal life as the immortality of our invisible souls. While our bodies may decay in their caskets or urns, the immaterial part of us lives on. But the story of Jesus' ascension insists otherwise: if Jesus will return to earth in the same way in which he departed (Acts 1:11), then he is and will remain an embodied human person. Once incarnate, always incarnate, we might say, which is why John's Gospel makes that scene with Thomas so prominent: the body that was crucified, the body with the scars from the nails, is the body Jesus has now—though it is, as Wright reminds us, *transphysical*.

Finally, we should also acknowledge that the ascension is tinged with sadness. The Feast of the Ascension, as one Catholic theologian has written, is a "festival of holy pain."[14] It comes near the end of the Easter season, and it marks the memory of Jesus' departure from this world—his "real absence," as is sometimes said. The Gospel of John records these words from Jesus' last evening with his disciples before his arrest and crucifixion: "I am going to him who sent me; yet none of you asks me, 'Where are you going?' But because I have said these things to you, sorrow has filled your hearts" (16:5-6). We long to see Jesus, to touch him, to be touched by him. But in a severely concrete sense, we can't do that now, at least not directly. So while we feast in honor of his exaltation, we also experience the ache of separation as we wonder what it means to keep following a risen Lord we can't see and talk with in the way his disciples were able to do as they followed him around Galilee.

I grew up hearing the story of Easter from before I knew how to talk, but I only noticed Matthew 28:16-17 (RSV) when I was a teenager: "Now [after Jesus' resurrection] the eleven disciples went to Galilee, to the mountain to which Jesus had directed them. When they saw him, they

worshiped him; but some doubted."[15] What did it mean,
I wondered with a sense of shock and scandal, that some
of Jesus' followers who saw with their own eyes that he
was alive . . . *doubted?*

It was Philip Yancey's book *The Jesus I Never Knew*
that first drew my attention to this unsettling moment
in the post-Easter appearances of Jesus. Yancey pro-
vided what I now know is a common way to understand
this "doubt":

> The Gospels portray Jesus' followers themselves as
> the ones most leery of rumors about a risen Jesus.
> One disciple especially, "doubting Thomas," has
> gained the reputation as a skeptic, but in truth all
> the disciples showed a lack of faith. None of them
> believed the wild report the women brought back
> from the empty tomb; "nonsense" they called it.
> Even after Jesus appeared to them in person, says
> Matthew, "some doubted." The eleven, whom Jesus
> had to rebuke for a stubborn refusal to believe, can
> hardly be called gullible.[16]

One could, as Yancey seems to do, spin this moment as
a positive one for apologetic purposes. By refusing easy

comfort, the doubting disciples demand more solid proofs, thereby fortifying the faith of us who believe in later times, in the absence of the firsthand encounter they had. Alternatively, one could use Matthew's brief narrative to underscore the ultimate insufficiency of "eyewitness testimony": if even the ones who saw the risen Jesus on a mountainside in Galilee could struggle to believe, then we too can breathe a bit easier, knowing that when we doubt, we're in good company and no worse off than the first generation of Christian believers.

If we look more carefully at Matthew's Greek text, however, the meaning of the disciples' doubt becomes less clear. The RSV translation makes it sound as if the disciples are divided into two groups: those who worshiped Jesus, and those (others) who doubted. But, as Walter Moberly points out in his book *The Bible, Theology and Faith*, the Greek syntax does not favor this interpretation.[17] It's likelier that the subject of the two verbs— "worshiped" and "doubted"—is the same group and that that group is the entire company of those who meet Jesus on the mountain. This explains why the New Revised Standard Version Updated Edition differs from the RSV: "When they saw him, they worshiped him, but they doubted." All those who worshiped also doubted, and vice versa.

Moberly proposes one further tweak, though. He asks whether "doubted" is the best way to render the verb *distazo* in English, since in the one other place in Matthew's Gospel where it appears (14:31), it suggests a certain flailing or uncertainty, rather than skepticism. So Moberly translates Matthew 28:17: "When [the disciples] saw [Jesus] they reverently prostrated themselves. But they were hesitant."[18]

Why would the disciples, in the presence of the risen Christ, be hesitant or uncertain? Centuries of Christian tradition have surely blunted our ability to appreciate the sheer strangeness and shock of one faithful Jew being raised from the dead in advance of the hoped-for general resurrection of all the dead at the culmination of history. Many of Jesus' contemporaries, schooled in the prophecies of Isaiah and Daniel, were eagerly anticipating the latter; none were expecting the former. And so the earliest witnesses of the risen Jesus were confused about what it should mean for them, what it obligated them to say or do. Should they go back to their fishing and hunker down in Galilee for a few more weeks or months (surely not years?) until Jesus returned to establish his kingship? Or . . . what exactly? Given the bizarreness of Easter morning, just what *was* the appropriate response?

Maybe this hesitation can help us better understand the assurance, joy, and boldness that came with the end of Jesus' resurrection appearances and the arrival of the Spirit on the day of Pentecost. If seeing Jesus alive brought a kind of happy but hesitant hope, it was what happened next that solidified the disciples' faith and galvanized their missionary proclamation. With the presence of the Spirit, it became unmistakably clear that Jesus had been raised and exalted not for some arcane purpose but precisely so that he could be present in a newly empowering, comforting way. "All authority in heaven and on earth has been given to me," Jesus said before his return to his Father. "Go therefore and make disciples of all nations, baptizing them in the name of the Father and of the Son and of the Holy Spirit, and teaching them to obey everything that I have commanded you. And remember, I am with you always, to the end of the age" (Matthew 28:18-20).

According to Luke, that is exactly what happened ten days later: Jesus' hesitant followers did remember—with palpable signs and wonders—that he would be with them, and they did begin to go out from Jerusalem to baptize new converts and make disciples.

It's to that Pentecostal zeal—the climactic, joyful theme of the Easter season—that we now turn in conclusion.

Conclusion

"Let Him Easter in Us"

To get to the place in Jerusalem where, since at least the fourth century, pilgrims have gone to venerate the site of Jesus' crucifixion and burial, you have to wend your way through a maze of narrow streets in the Christian Quarter of the old city. In the first century, this area would have been a desolate hill outside the city walls. But now it is a honeycomb of limestone buildings and awning-shadowed byways crammed with hawkers, tourists, police officers, and religious seekers.

When you reach the Church of the Holy Sepulchre, you have to proceed inside to a smaller structure—about the size of one of those North Pole houses where children go to meet Santa Claus inside shopping malls—if you want to access the place where Joseph of Arimathea is said to have hastily laid Jesus' corpse before the sunset signaled the beginning of the Sabbath (Matthew 27:59-60). You will wait in line for a while, depending on the time of day, as pilgrim after pilgrim files into the *edicule*, as it's called (the Roman term for a small shrine). Once inside, you find that you are in a kind of foyer or antechamber lit only by a handful of candles. This is the Chapel of the Angel, in honor of the messenger who announced to the women, "He is not here, for he has been raised." You are not yet to the place of Jesus' burial. You will wait a few minutes for those ahead of you.

When it's your turn, you have to stoop to pass through a low doorway (the architecture mandates reverence) to see the place where Jesus' body lay. Only four people can fit into this space—"the holiest shrine in Christendom [is] the size of a small broom cupboard"[1]—and you have less than half a minute to reverence the vacant marble slab before you need to exit and make room for the pilgrims behind you. Your eye may linger on the relief sculpture in which the angels' words are carved: "Who do you seek? Are you seeking Jesus of Nazareth, who was crucified? He has risen, he is not here; see the place where they laid him."

Once you leave the edicule, you're back in the larger church, and your angle of vision is suddenly expanded. You merge with the chaotic, noisy crowd that is swarming in all directions. Up to that point, it was as if you were descending into an ever-dimmer cone: from the streets of the old city, into the church, into the edicule, into the chapel, and finally into the cramped space of the empty place where Jesus is no more. Now you are propelled outward into the teeming, thronging wider world, somehow to try to assimilate what you've just seen and experienced into your regular life. You pat your pocket to make sure you didn't leave your phone in the chamber, you regroup with your fellow pilgrims, you leave the church and make your way back to the hotel where you're staying.

Now what will you do?

According to the Acts of the Apostles, fifty days after Jesus' resurrection, Jerusalem was abuzz the way it always is now. Thousands of pilgrims had converged on the city for the annual celebration of Shavuot, the Feast of Weeks

(*Pentēcostē hēmera* in Greek—the fiftieth day after the second day of Passover) to mark the time of the wheat harvest. There were "Parthians, Medes, Elamites, and residents of Mesopotamia, Judea and Cappadocia, Pontus and Asia, Phrygia and Pamphylia, Egypt and the parts of Libya belonging to Cyrene, and visitors from Rome, both Jews and proselytes, Cretans and Arabs" (Acts 2:9-11)— the whole panoply of human races and cultures, no less varied and colorful in its era than the one you find in Jerusalem to this day.

Ten days earlier, in Luke's telling, Jesus' disciples had watched him ascend into the sky and disappear behind a cloud (Acts 1:6-11). Now they were together in one place, and "suddenly from heaven there came a sound like the rush of a violent wind, and it filled the entire house where they were sitting. Divided tongues, as of fire, appeared among them, and a tongue rested on each of them. All of them were filled with the Holy Spirit and began to speak in other languages, as the Spirit gave them ability" (Acts 2:2-4).

To interpret this strange occurrence, Peter stands up and preaches to the crowds of pilgrims: "This Jesus God raised up, and of that all of us are witnesses. Being therefore exalted at the right hand of God and having received from the Father the promise of the Holy Spirit, he has poured out this that you both see and hear" (Acts 2:32-33). Here and now, Peter says, in effect, is the crowning work of the entire history of God's saving action on our behalf.

The redemption of the world, begun before the foundation of the world, inaugurated in Bethlehem, accomplished on the cross, confirmed in the ascension and enthronement of Christ, is fulfilled in the sending of the Spirit, and all the components of the great work are at last in place.[2]

Although, since the ascension, believers no longer enjoy the visible presence of Jesus, we now have the comforting and empowering presence of his Spirit to guide us into truer understanding and to impel us out into the world for mission and service.

One of my favorite pieces of artwork is a painting by the English artist Sir Stanley Spencer (1891–1959). Spencer lived in the village of Cookham, south of Oxford and east of London, and his 1924–1927 piece *Resurrection, Cookham* depicts a church graveyard with a diverse crowd of people emerging from their tombs. The painting is massive—over nine by sixteen feet—and its exquisite details invite you to linger with it. In the shadow of the church, the risen Jesus sits under an archway of white flowers, with God the Father standing behind him. Although the setting is contemporary, Moses is one of the newly risen. With his tasseled robe, he stands alongside nondescript English villagers who help each other brush dirt from their clothes and who recline like sunbathers on their tombstones. The scene is familiar, homely: you can imagine the painting's subjects, once they recover from the shock of no longer being underground, deciding to walk to the market to purchase food for a picnic. The whole painting suggests, in the words of one critic, that "the resurrection can come to any man (or woman) at any time, and consists in being aware of the real meaning of life and alive to its enormous possibilities."[3] The painting invites the question, what does it mean to live out a resurrected existence right here, right now? If I have been raised with Christ, what difference does that make to my life in the world?

When I was new to the liturgical traditions of the church, I remember attending a service on the day of Pentecost and being charmed by the almost childlike exuberance of the customs on display. Most of the congregants were wearing firetruck-red shirts, sweaters, or hats, recalling the flames that danced on the heads of the disciples in Jerusalem. The opening processional from the rear of the church to the high altar involved someone holding aloft on a long, bendable wand a shiny silken kite in the form of a dove. Like a conductor, they waved the wand back and forth, the kite swooping and soaring this way and that, as the congregation sang:

> Hail this joyful day's return,
> hail the Pentecostal morn,
> morn when our ascended Lord
> on his church his Spirit poured!
> Like to cloven tongues of flame
> on the Twelve the Spirit came—
> tongues, that earth may hear their call,
> fire, that love may burn in all.[4]

If the Feast of the Ascension carries a whiff of sadness with it, we can't say the same about Pentecost. Here, finally, is what Jesus promised—that as he removes himself from our sight, he does not thereby leave us alone and adrift. His Spirit—his "unbodily personal power," as Dallas Willard memorably called it—will continue to enliven, surprise, and sustain us until he returns to make all things new. What this last great feast day of the Easter season means, in the words of priest and scholar Gerhard Lohfink, is that we are all

> anticipating that at every hour the Spirit of Christ will show the community new paths, expecting new doors to open at any moment, counting on it that at any hour the Spirit can transform evil into good, hoping at every hour that the impossible will become possible, and never saying "later!" but always "now!"[5]

As another Catholic priest, the nineteenth-century Jesuit poet Gerard Manley Hopkins prayed, "Let him easter in us, be a dayspring to the dimness of us, be a crimson-cresseted east."[6]

Although there are a thousand different ways to answer the question of how the Spirit of the risen Jesus makes Easter come alive again and again in and among us, I want to mention just four in conclusion.

First, *understanding Jesus.* In his farewell discourses in the Gospel of John, Jesus promised that after he was raised and had ascended to the Father, his Spirit would guide his followers into a deeper apprehension of all that he had revealed to them during his earthly ministry: "The Advocate, the Holy Spirit, whom the Father will send in my name, will teach you everything, and remind you of all that I have said to you" (John 14:26). One of the striking features of the Gospel stories is how uncomprehending Jesus' disciples are throughout the entirety of his earthly life. They misunderstand his mission and teaching at every turn. Only after his crucifixion and resurrection do they find their eyes opening and insight dawning. This new understanding is the fruit of Pentecost: Jesus' own Spirit leads his followers to comb back through their memories, shedding fresh light on all that Jesus said and did, and showing how it all culminated on that frightful and happy Sunday morning in Jerusalem. And, the New Testament implies, this journey of deepening understanding is ongoing. We today are still caught up, by and with the Spirit, in trying to comprehend the vastness and depth of the love that Jesus demonstrated. And we will be for the remainder of our lives—and beyond.

Second, *finding hope.* When the great theologian Jürgen Moltmann was sixteen years old in 1943, he was drafted into the German army and was soon captured by the Allied forces. He wound up in a prisoner of war camp in Scotland and, having had no religious upbringing, was given a Bible by a chaplain. Moltmann later said he would have preferred to have been given some cigarettes. Nonetheless, he started reading the Bible in the evenings in his barracks, returning again and again to the Gospel of Mark. In particular, he found himself mesmerized by Jesus' cry of dereliction from the cross: "My God, my God, why hast thou forsaken me?" (Mark 15:34 KJV). Looking back on the experience, Moltmann would write, "I felt growing within me the conviction: this is someone who understands you completely, who is with you in your cry to God and has felt the same forsakenness you are living in now." But Moltmann also came to believe that this Godforsaken crucified man wasn't just a sympathetic character in a story, like a protagonist in a novel who makes you feel better understood but ultimately can't offer you any real friendship. No, Moltmann came to believe that this fellow sufferer who understood him was presently alive and able to relate to him. From the vantage point of sixty years, Moltmann said, "I am certain that then, in 1945, and there, in the Scottish prisoner of war camp, in the dark pit of my soul, Jesus sought me and found me. 'He came to seek that which was lost,' and so he came to me when I was lost."[7] He came to Moltmann by his Spirit, and he comes to lost souls today in the same way. That, too, is the meaning of Easter and Pentecost.

Third, *discovering purpose.* By the time any of us arrive at the age when we're able to read a book like this one, we have become painfully aware of the apparent chaos and ruthless, cruel disappointments of life. We fall in love, only to watch our beloved die from a rare incurable illness. We work diligently to prepare for a career we feel we were born to have, only to see it torpedoed by a false accusation or a simple avoidable mistake. None of us make it to adulthood, unless we're very lucky, without slamming into the brutal truth that there is apparently no upward trajectory in life, no arc of history we can rely on to bend toward justice. Which means that, to the clear-eyed, coldly realistic among us, nihilistic despair seems to be the only rational response to the world. And yet . . .

When Lesslie Newbigin, the famous twentieth-century ecumenist and missionary bishop to India, was asked in an interview whether he was hopeful or despairing about the effects of his ministry, he replied, "I am neither an optimist nor a pessimist. Jesus Christ is risen from the dead!"[8] The conclusions we are able to draw simply from observing the world in all its anarchy and pain will never tell the full story. Sunny optimism or despairing pessimism can't be our only options if Jesus, the friend of sinners and sufferers, is alive. To adapt some words from Uncle Screwtape: to look around upon a universe from which every trace of him seems to have vanished, and ask why you have been forsaken, and still to hope—this is the kind of durable purpose and motivation the Spirit grants us through the Easter message.[9]

Fourth, *persevering in prayer*. If all this is true—if above and in and through the messy reality of history is the risen Jesus—then we can speak to him with the confidence that he is with us and will always act on our behalf. The Spirit intercedes for us even when we run out of words, says the apostle Paul, and he does this because he is Jesus' Spirit, and Jesus "always lives to make intercession for [us]" (Hebrews 7:25; see also Romans 8:26-27, 34).

Theologian Robert Jenson writes about petitionary prayer:

All actual occasions occur not mechanistically determined but in freedom, and this freedom is the freedom not of mere chance but of a spirit. It is the freedom of the risen Lord's freedom, of the Holy Spirit, of the very Spirit we address in both petition and praise. The arrow of time is Jesus' breath.[10]

Prayer, then, is our asking for what we need from the one who has triumphed over the world's processes of decay and disorientation. We aren't trapped by the limited options of life as we've always known it. Jesus is alive, and he exhales healing, vitality, and wholeness into our world. His Spirit is with us.

The Lord is risen! The Lord is risen indeed! Alleluia!

Acknowledgments

I am grateful to Esau McCaulley for inviting me to contribute to this series and for his vision and encouragement. In the initial planning stages, Ethan McCarthy, formerly at InterVarsity Press, offered help with his characteristic gentleness and wisdom.

My research assistants at Western Theological Seminary, Nick Rogalski and AJ Funk, tracked down numerous sources for me and stimulated my thinking through many conversations. My faculty colleagues at Western, especially Winn Collier, Kristen Johnson, and Suzanne McDonald, stepped in with timely help at crucial moments.

Todd Billings, Andy McCoy, and Benj Petroelje did me the honor of reading through portions of the first three chapters and cheered me on. And audiences at the Episcopal Church of the Incarnation in Dallas, Texas, responded with warm encouragement as I tried out ideas in an adult education forum. I am grateful to the Rt. Rev. Tony Burton and the Rev. Christopher Beeley for the invitation to serve for a time as a Visiting Scripture Scholar at Incarnation.

Some of the writing was done at Laity Lodge in Texas, a place where I have found a lot of solace and respite in recent years. I am grateful to Steven Purcell and the entire team—friends, all—at Laity for their matchless hospitality.

And I am especially appreciative of Ted Olsen, my editor at InterVarsity Press, whose patience throughout the writing process was herculean.

This book was written during a season of acute personal difficulty. For support and friendship throughout, I am thankful for Mike Allen, Gary Beson, Sarah Dahl, Russell Hilliard, Joe Lawrence, Jono Linebaugh, Jeb Ralston, James Schetelich, Jamie Sosnowski, Joseph Tay, and the Smith family.

This book is dedicated with love to my godson Solomon Everett Smith. May you grow up, Solomon, always knowing the truth and hope of the Easter good news, the Love who lives for you with death behind him.

Notes

INTRODUCTION: THE PASSOVER OF THE LORD

[1] In Western, English-speaking Christianity, we often refer to the week leading up to Easter as "Passion Week," from the Greek word *paschein,* which means "to suffer." However, despite an ancient tradition, *pascha* and *paschein* are not etymologically related. See Melito of Sardis, *On Pascha*, 2nd ed. (Yonkers, NY: St. Vladimir's Seminary Press, 2016), 63, 65.

[2] The preacher was the Bishop of Durham at the time, N. T. Wright. His sermon from that service can be read at "Dreaming of a White Easter," N. T. Wright Online, 2008, https://ntwrightpage.com/2016/03/30 /dreaming-of-a-white-easter. The book he wrote is *The Resurrection of the Son of God*, Christian Origins and the Question of God, vol. 3 (Minneapolis, MN: Fortress, 2003). It is eminently worth reading, though some have rightly noted that for all the carefulness of Wright's historical investigations, the resurrection isn't something that can be proved by research, no matter how rigorous. See further George Hunsinger, "The Third Day He Rose Again from the Dead: *Tertia dia resurrexit a mortuis*," in *Exploring and Proclaiming the Apostles' Creed*, ed. Roger E. Van Harn (Grand Rapids, MI: Eerdmans, 2004), 136-53.

[3] Philip H. Pfatteicher, *Journey into the Heart of God: Living the Liturgical Year* (Oxford, UK: Oxford University Press, 2013), 215.

[4] Beth Maynard, "Waiting for the Light," *The Living Church*, February 7, 2010, 15-17, https://archive.theadventboston.org/tlclight.pdf.

[5] Clement of Alexandria, as quoted in Pfatteicher, *Journey into the Heart of God*, 215.

[6] Maynard, "Waiting for the Light."

[7] Aidan Kavanagh, *Elements of Rite: A Handbook of Liturgical Style* (Collegeville, MN: Liturgical Press, 1982), 28.

[8] Book of Common Prayer, 1979, 374.

1. The First Easter

[1] "Faith and theology ask, 'Who is Jesus?' because the primal proclamation of the gospel, 'Jesus is risen,' is a simple subject-predicate proposition, with the personal name 'Jesus' as the subject. That the gospel is indeed gospel [i.e., *good*, as opposed to bad, news] therefore depends on who Jesus is; the proposition 'Stalin is risen' would not be good news for many. 'The unconditional friend of publicans and sinners is risen' is good news to anyone willing to try those shoes on; 'the chief keeper of the gulag is risen' would be good news to very few." Robert W. Jenson, "Identity, Jesus, and Exegesis," in *Seeking the Identity of Jesus: A Pilgrimage,* ed. Beverly Roberts Gaventa and Richard B. Hays (Grand Rapids, MI: Eerdmans, 2008), 43.

[2] In most Bibles, another eleven verses come after this disquieting end. But the consensus among textual scholars is that these verses were added later by someone other than the original Gospel writer.

[3] Russell Moore (@drmoore), "Most hilarious line in all Bible is Matt 27:65, Pilate on the tomb of Jesus: 'Go, make it as secure as you can.' Good luck with that," X, April 19, 2014, 12:05 p.m., https://x.com/drmoore/status/457550624515948545.

[4] Dale C. Allison, *The Resurrection of Jesus: Apologetics, Polemics, History* (London: Bloomsbury, 2021), 3, emphasis added.

[5] In Franco Zeffirelli's 1977 film and TV miniseries *Jesus of Nazareth,* which I probably watched a dozen times in my childhood, the two angels are depicted as white-garbed gardeners, tilling the ground with spades. With flat affects and ironic detachment, they stop their hoeing, perplexed, and mutter to the women an expansive paraphrase of those words from Luke: "Where are you going? Why seek the living among the dead? Jesus is not there." It's a haunting, unsettling dramatization, thanks in large part to the musical soundtrack, which one writer describes like this: "The eerie electronic notes of a Theremin over a low percussive rumble underscore the sense of the uncanny. The women hurry on to the tomb, only to find it empty. They run back, full of questions, to where they saw the gardeners, but now the hillside is empty. Only a couple of hoes remain as tangible signs that this was more than a vision." Jim Friedrich, "Cinematic Resurrections

(Part 1)," *The Religious Imagineer* (blog), April 10, 2016, https://jimfriedrich.com/tag/resurrection-in-zeffirellis-jesus-of-nazareth-movie.

6 Who were the two disciples? Could "Cleopas" be the same person as "Clopas" mentioned in John 19:25, whose wife, Mary, stood near the cross and saw Jesus die? If so, it may be that the other disciple whom Luke does not name is this Mary. To make things more interesting, the early church historian Eusebius claims that Cleopas (or Clopas) was the brother of Joseph, husband of the virgin Mary. Might Jesus have been walking on the road with his uncle and aunt?

7 There may be an evocation here of the imagery of the Ark of the Covenant in Israel's tabernacle and temple, in which the golden mercy seat is flanked by two winged angels (cherubim) (Exodus 25:17-22). Throughout the Old Testament, God is described as the one who sits or dwells in the place between the cherubim (1 Samuel 4:4; 2 Samuel 6:2; 2 Kings 19:15; 1 Chronicles 13:6; Psalm 80:1; Psalm 99:1; Isaiah 37:16). Might it be that John's Gospel is gesturing toward the empty tomb as the "place" where we see— or, rather, now don't see but still encounter—the God of Israel? See Rowan Williams, *On Christian Theology* (Oxford: Blackwell, 2000), 186-87.

8 I know of no more powerful discussion of this theme than that found in Rowan Williams, *Resurrection: Interpreting the Easter Gospel* (Cleveland, OH: Pilgrim, 2002 [1982]), 30: "To be present to myself before the risen Jesus is to be present to God, and to know that the presence signifies mercy, acceptance and hope."

9 This is Francis Spufford's summary of the Easter gospel in *Unapologetic: Why, Despite Everything, Christianity Can Still Make Surprising Emotional Sense* (New York: HarperOne, 2013), 146.

2. "We Shall Also Live with Him"

1 Aidan Kavanagh, "A Rite of Passage," *Call to Worship* 36, no. 2 (2002–2003): 23.

2 Early Christians took off their clothes before being baptized and then received a white robe when they emerged from the pool. Everyone's robe looked the same, underscoring the point Paul makes in Galatians: "As many of you as were baptized into Christ have clothed yourselves with Christ. There is no longer Jew or Greek, there is no longer slave or free, there is no longer male and female; for all of you are one in Christ Jesus. And if you belong to Christ, then you are Abraham's offspring, heirs according to the promise" (3:27-29). To this day in the Church of England's *Common*

Worship baptismal liturgy, "Provision is made for clothing [in a white robe] after the baptism." "Baptism and Confirmation," The Church of England, www.churchofengland.org/prayer-and-worship/worship-texts -and-resources/common-worship/christian-initiation/baptism-and, accessed July 5, 2024.

3 Alexander Schmemann, *Of Water and the Spirit: A Liturgical Study of Baptism* (Crestwood, NY: St. Vladimir's Seminary Press, 1974), 7.

4 For a rich discussion of these and many other passages in the Hebrew Bible, see Jon D. Levenson, *Resurrection and the Restoration of Israel: The Ultimate Victory of the God of Life* (New Haven, CT: Yale University Press, 2008), and Kevin J. Madigan and Jon D. Levenson, *Resurrection: The Power of God for Christians and Jews* (New Haven, CT: Yale University Press, 2008).

5 Robert W. Jenson, *The Triune Identity: God According to the Gospel* (Philadelphia: Fortress, 1982), 44.

6 "The fact that baptism could be construed as a symbolic burial with Christ (Rom. 6:4; Col. 2:12) suggests a complete immersion in water," rather than affusion. Wayne Meeks, *The First Urban Christians: The Social World of the Apostle Paul*, 2nd ed. (New Haven, CT: Yale University Press, 2002), 150.

7 Martin Luther, *Large Catechism,* 4.65.

8 Book of Common Prayer, 1979, 306.

9 Douglas A. Campbell, *Pauline Dogmatics: The Triumph of God's Love* (Grand Rapids, MI: Eerdmans, 2020), 206.

10 Book of Common Prayer, 1979, 305-6.

11 John Calvin, *Institutes of the Christian Religion*, 2 vols., trans. Ford Lewis Battles, ed. John T. McNeill (Louisville, KY: Westminster John Knox, 2006), 4.15.4, 1306-7.

12 For a wonderful contemporary (Western) use of this iconographic tradition, see the graphic novel by Evan Dahm, *The Harrowing of Hell* (Chicago: Iron Circus Comics, 2020).

3. "Thou Wast Up by Break of Day"

1 See Jean Daniélou, *The Bible and the Liturgy* (Notre Dame, IN: Notre Dame Press, 1956), chaps. 15–16.

2 Book of Common Prayer, 1979, 363.

3 John Behr, *John the Theologian and His Paschal Gospel: A Prologue to Theology* (Oxford, UK: Oxford University Press, 2019).

4 N. T. Wright, "Dreaming of a White Easter," N. T. Wright Online, 2008, https:// ntwrightpage.com/2016/03/30/dreaming-of-a-white-easter.

5 Wright, "Dreaming of a White Easter."

6 Wright, "Dreaming of a White Easter."

7 The first Easter Vigil service I attended was at the Church of the Resurrection, at that time meeting in a school auditorium in Glen Ellyn, Illinois, when I was in college. It began after dark in the evening, and it was at least 2 a.m. by the time it finished. There were streamers, banners, laughter, and dancing on the stage and in the aisles. It was a full-on, no-holds-barred party. I've never forgotten it.

8 Of course all human festivals, this side of the total victory of Easter, still have a dark side. One wonders what all the slaves were doing when their masters were attending services. Medieval Christians used Holy Week leading up to Easter to persecute Jews. Even the celebration of Jesus' self-giving love can apparently become the occasion for self-serving violence and exclusion. On this whole problem, see Lauren F. Winner, *The Dangers of Christian Practice: On Wayward Gifts, Characteristic Damage, and Sin* (New Haven, CT: Yale University Press, 2018).

9 Sarah Puryear, "Living All Fifty Days of the Easter Season," The Living Church, April 18, 2024, https://livingchurch.org/covenant/living-all-fifty -days-of-the-easter-season.

10 Robert Farrar Capon, *The Supper of the Lamb: A Culinary Reflection* (New York: Modern Library, 2002 [1969]). See also Rev. Leo Patalinghug and Michael P. Foley, *Dining with the Saints: The Sinner's Guide to a Righteous Feast* (Washington, DC: Regnery, 2023); Michael P. Foley, *Drinking with the Saints: The Sinner's Guide to a Holy Happy Hour* (Washington, DC: Regnery, 2022); and Alexander Greeley and Fernando Flores, *Cooking with the Saints* (Bedford, NH: Sophia Institute Press, 2019).

11 David Cobb and Derek Olsen, eds., *Saint Augustine's Prayer Book: A Book of Devotions* (Cincinnati, OH: Forward Movement, 2014), 285. See also Raymond Chapman, *Stations of the Resurrection: Meditations on the Fourteen Resurrection Appearances* (Harrisburg, PA: Morehouse, 1998). There is also a series of audio meditations available online for private or small group use at "Via Lucis: The Stations of the Resurrection," Formed, https://watch .formed.org/via-lucis, accessed July 6, 2024.

12 This homily is widely available in multiple translations online. For the version quoted here, see John Chrysostom, "The Easter Sermon of John Chrysostom," Fordham University, April 1996, https://origin-rh.web .fordham.edu/Halsall/source/chrysostom-easter.asp.

[13] For the poem and insightful commentary on it, see John Drury, *Music at Midnight: The Life and Poetry of George Herbert* (Chicago: University of Chicago Press, 2013), 143.

4. World Upside Down

[1] Nicholas Kristof, "Reverend, You Say the Virgin Birth is 'a Bizarre Claim'?" *New York Times*, April 20, 2019, www.nytimes.com/2019/04/20/opinion /sunday/christian-easter-serene-jones.html.

[2] Andrew McGowan (@BerkeleyDean), "If Easter really meant just that love is more powerful than death but Jesus didn't rise, how's the love-death score today? Is it coincidental that liberal Protestantism grows in the soil of privilege? #SriLanka," X, April 21, 2019, 11:34 a.m., https://twitter.com /BerkeleyDean/status/1119987867923644422.

[3] These opening paragraphs of chap. 4 are adapted and used with permission from Wesley Hill, "After Boomer Religion," *Commonweal*, April 29, 2019, www.commonwealmagazine.org/after-boomer-religion.

[4] Robert Morgan and Patrick Moule, eds., *Christ Alive and at Large: The Unpublished Writings of C. F. D. Moule* (London: Canterbury Press Norwich, 2010).

[5] As quoted in Jürgen Moltmann, *The Way of Jesus Christ: Christology in Messianic Dimensions* (Minneapolis, MN: Fortress, 1995), 29.

[6] John R. W. Stott, *Basic Christianity* (London: Inter-Varsity Press, 1958), 23.

[7] "The Lausanne Covenant," Lausanne Movement, 1974, https://lausanne .org/statement/lausanne-covenant.

[8] John Stott, "The Lausanne Covenant: An Exposition and Commentary by John Stott," Lausanne Movement, 1975, https://lausanne.org/occasional -paper/lop-3.

[9] For an introduction to Scudder's life and vision, see Jonathan McGregor, "A Rich Woman Who Took the Magnificat Seriously," *The Christian Century*, December 11, 2023, www.christiancentury.org/features/rich-woman -who-took-magnificat-seriously.

[10] Vida Dutton Scudder, *Social Teachings of the Christian Year*, Library of Anglican Theology (Galesburg, IL: Seminary Street Press, 2022 [1918]), 118.

[11] Scudder, *Social Teachings*, 122-23.

[12] Scudder, *Social Teachings*, 118.

5. The Right Hand of God

1 The 1980 *Jesus Film*, produced by the college ministry CRU (formerly Campus Crusade for Christ), shows this scene from Jesus' point of view. We see a wind rustling the disciples' hair and clothes, but instead of a cloud obscuring Jesus from their sight, we see clouds obscuring them from Jesus' sight.

2 Book of Common Prayer, 1979, 226.

3 J. G. Davies, *He Ascended into Heaven* (London: Lutterworth, 1989), 9.

4 Marva Dawn and Eugene Peterson, *The Unnecessary Pastor: Rediscovering the Call* (Grand Rapids, MI: Eerdmans, 1999), 140, 144-45.

5 Douglas Farrow, *Ascension Theology* (London: Bloomsbury, 2011), 16.

6 James Alison, *Knowing Jesus* (London: SPCK, 1998), 19.

7 Luke Timothy Johnson, *The Real Jesus: The Misguided Quest for the Historical Jesus and the Truth of the Traditional Gospels* (San Francisco: HarperOne, 1997), 134.

8 Athanasius, *Against the Arians*, 1.61.

9 The image of the "Father's right hand" comes from Psalm 110:1: "The LORD says to my lord, 'Sit at my right hand until I make your enemies your footstool.'" No Old Testament passage is quoted or alluded to in the New Testament more frequently than this one.

10 N. T. Wright, *Surprised by Hope: Rethinking Heaven, the Resurrection, and the Mission of the Church* (New York: HarperCollins, 2008), 44.

11 Paul J. Griffiths, *Christian Flesh* (Stanford, CA: Stanford University Press, 2018), 47.

12 Charles Wesley, "Love's Redeeming Work is Done," *The Hymnal 1982* (New York: Church Hymnal Corporation, 1985), no. 188.

13 Farrow, *Ascension Theology*, 34.

14 Karl Rahner, *Theological Investigations*, vol. 5 (New York: Crossroad, 1970), 171.

15 This and the following paragraphs previously appeared in Wesley Hill, "Easter Hesitation and Pentecostal Hope," *Covenant*, The Living Church, May 16, 2024, https://livingchurch.org/covenant/easter-hesitation-and-pentecostal-hope/.

16 Philip Yancey, *The Jesus I Never Knew* (Grand Rapids, MI: Zondervan, 1995), 212.

17 R. W. L. Moberly, *The Bible, Theology and Faith: A Study of Abraham and Jesus*, CSCD (Cambridge, UK: Cambridge University Press, 2000), 191-2.

18 Moberly, *The Bible, Theology and Faith*, 192.

Conclusion: "Let Him Easter in Us"

[1] William Dalrymple, *In Xanadu: A Quest* (New York: Vintage, 1990), 4.

[2] Philip H. Pfatteicher, *Journey into the Heart of God: Living the Liturgical Year* (Oxford, UK: Oxford University Press, 2013), 267.

[3] W. G. Hall, quoted in Keith Bell, *Stanley Spencer* (London: Phaidon, 1992), 59.

[4] Hilary of Poitiers, "Hail this Joyful Day's Return," *The Hymnal 1982* (New York: Church Hymnal Corporation, 1985), no. 223.

[5] Gerhard Lohfink, *Jesus of Nazareth: What He Wanted, Who He Was* (Collegeville, MN: Liturgical Press, 2015), 306.

[6] Gerard Manley Hopkins, "The Wreck of the Deutschland," in *The Poems of Gerard Manley Hopkins*, 4th ed., ed. W. H. Gardner and N. H. Mackenzie (London: Oxford University Press, 1967), 63.

[7] Jürgen Moltmann, *A Broad Place: An Autobiography* (Minneapolis, MN: Fortress, 2009), 30.

[8] Quoted in N. T. Wright, *Pauline Perspectives: Essays on Paul, 1978–2013* (Minneapolis, MN: Fortress, 2013), 269.

[9] C. S. Lewis, *The Screwtape Letters* (New York: HarperCollins, 2001), 40.

[10] Robert W. Jenson, *The Trinity and the Spirit: Two Essays from Christian Dogmatics* (Minneapolis, MN: Fortress, 2023), 209.

The Fullness of Time Series

Each volume in the Fullness of Time series invites readers to engage with the riches of the church year, exploring the traditions, prayers, Scriptures, and rituals of the seasons of the church calendar.

LENT

Esau McCaulley

CHRISTMAS

Emily Hunter McGowin

EASTER

Wesley Hill

EPIPHANY

Fleming Rutledge

PENTECOST

Emilio Alvarez

ORDINARY TIME

Amy Peeler

ADVENT

Tish Harrison Warren

Like this book?
Scan the code to discover more content like this!

Get on IVP's email list to receive special offers, exclusive book news, and thoughtful content from your favorite authors on topics you care about.

 InterVarsity Press